TEACHER'S EDITION

LATIN AND GREEK ROOTS:
A STUDY OF WORD FAMILIES

IV

By: Elizabeth Osborne

Edited by Paul Moliken
Illustrated by Larry Knox

Prestwick House wishes to extend its gratitude to the many contributors whose assistance, comments, and expertise were essential in completing this book.

PH PRESTWICK HOUSE, INC.
"Everything for the English Classroom!"

P.O. Box 658 • Clayton, DE 19938
Tel: 1.800.932.4593 • Web site: www.prestwickhouse.com

ISBN: 978-1-60389-128-8

INTRODUCTION

Prestwick House developed *Vocabulary from Latin and Greek Roots* in response to numerous requests for a solid etymology-based vocabulary program. Because the aim of the program is to increase retention of new words as well as to expand students' vocabulary, we chose to organize the Units by meaning rather than alphabetically. A student who associates a root with an idea will be more likely to correctly assess the definition of that root's English derivative.

Each Unit contains four Latin and/or Greek roots; two to four English vocabulary words are provided for each root. Unit 9 of this book (p. 54), for example, includes four roots having to do with rolling, twisting, and turning. When a student begins this Unit, he or she will see the key letters which signal the presence of the root in an English word: TORT. Beneath the key letters is the root from which the English is derived. Students will notice that there are sometimes two forms of the root. The inclusion of two forms indicates a Latin verb from which English has taken two different forms. TORQUERE, for instance, gives us the word *torque*, meaning "a twisting force," while TORTUS, another form of the verb, gives us *extort*, meaning "to twist (something) out of someone."

When a root comes from a Latin adjective or noun, only one form will generally be included. Greek roots also appear in only one form.

Beneath the definition of the root, the student will find the word, its pronunciation, part of speech, and English definition. In cases in which an English word has multiple meanings, we have chosen to include only the meaning appropriate to the grade level for which the book is intended. The word *temper* in this book, then, is a verb meaning "to make less severe," rather than the more familiar noun denoting a person's disposition or mood; in Book III, *pedestrian* means "ordinary" rather than "a traveler on foot." In some instances, students may find it useful to review meanings that do not appear and discuss how the meanings and definitions are related to the meaning presented.

If the word has a prefix, or if it is especially difficult to reconcile with its root, the entry will contain an analysis of the parts of the word, followed by a literal definition. *Retort* in Book IV, Unit Nine, is explained as *re*, meaning "back," + *tortus*; the literal meaning is "to twist (words) back."

Finally, each entry provides a sentence using the word and introduces pertinent synonyms and/or antonyms. For added visual reinforcement of this understanding, a mnemonic cartoon appears in each Unit.

Six different kinds of exercise follow the Unit entries. They include three kinds of practice using words in context, one test of a student's ability to infer information based on a word's meaning, one reading comprehension exercise, and one activity in which a student must deduce the meaning of an unfamiliar word based on knowledge of the word's root. By the end of the exercises in each Unit, students will have had thorough practice using the word in context and will be prepared to make the word part of their working vocabulary.

We hope that you find the *Vocabulary from Latin and Greek Roots* series effective in teaching new words and in fostering student interest in the history of our fascinating language.

Note: A guide to the pronunciation symbols and a list of Latin and Greek prefixes can be found at the beginning of this book.

PREFIXES

A (L.) away from	EN (G.) in, within
A (G.) not, no	EPI (G.) upon
AB (L.) away from	EX (L.) out of, away from *
AD (L.) toward	HYPER (G.) over
ALTER (L.) another	IN (L.) in, into, on, against, not
AMPHI (G.) around, both	INTRO (L.) inside
ANA (G.) up	OB (L.) against
ANTE (L.) before	OMNI (L.) every, all
ANTI (G.) against	PER (L.) through
CIRCUM (L.) around	PERI (G.) around
CO (L.) with, together	POST (L.) after
CON (L.) with, together	PRE (L.) before
CONTRA (L.) against	RE (L.) back, again *
DE (L.) down, down from	RETRO (L.) backwards
DIA (G.) through	SUB (L.) beneath
DIS (L.) apart, away from	SUPER, SUR (L.) above
DYS (G.) bad	SYM (G.) with, together
E (L.) out of	SYN (G.) with, together
EC (G.) outside	TRANS (L.) across
EM (G.) in, within	TELE (G.) distant

* Note: *Com, ex, in,* and *re* sometimes serve as *intensifiers*. In such cases, these prefixes simply mean *very*.

PRONUNCIATION GUIDE

a = tr<u>a</u>ck	o = j<u>o</u>b
ā = m<u>a</u>te	ō = wr<u>o</u>te
ä = f<u>a</u>ther	ô = p<u>o</u>rt
â = c<u>a</u>re	ōō = pr<u>oo</u>f
e = p<u>e</u>t	u = p<u>u</u>n
ē = b<u>e</u>	ū = <u>you</u>
	û = p<u>u</u>rr
i = b<u>i</u>t	
ī = b<u>i</u>te	ə = <u>a</u>bout, syst<u>e</u>m, s<u>u</u>pper, circ<u>u</u>s

WORD LIST FOR BOOK IV

Unit 1
conducive
deduce
evince
impetuous
impetus
induce
intractable
invincible
petulant
protracted
provincial
retract

Unit 2
anatomy
compunction
concise
dichotomy
epitome
excise
fractious
incisive
infraction
infringe
punctilious
pungent
tome

Unit 3
abject
compel
conjecture
dejected
dismissive
emissary
emote
expel
impulse
motif
motive
remiss

Unit 4
comportment
confer
defer
deference
deviate
impervious
inference
obviate
proffer
proliferate
purported
viaduct

Unit 5
apparition
aspect
diaphanous
envisage
epiphany
introspective
perspicacious
phenomenon
retrospective
sycophant
visage

Unit 6
adherent
diffuse
diligent
dissolute
effusive
incoherent
inherent
insoluble
profuse
recollect
resolute
sacrilege

Unit 7
constructive
construe
destitute
expound
facile
facsimile
factotum
infrastructure
proficient
proponent
restitution
stature

Unit 8
complacent
docile
doctrine
gratuitous
indoctrinate
ingrate
ingratiate
intemperate
placebo
placid
temper
temperance

Unit 9
adverse
convoluted
deflect
evolve
extort
inflection
inflexible
retort
revert
subvert
tortuous
voluble

Unit 10
approbation
culpable
culprit
decriminalize
exonerate
incriminate
mea culpa
onerous
onus
recrimination
reprobate
reprove

Unit 11
confide
credence
credible
credulity
diffident
dubious
fallacious
fallacy
fallible
fidelity
incredulous
indubitable
redoubtable

Unit 12
definitive
infinite
infinitesimal
innovative
novel
novice
penultimate
primacy
primal
primeval
ultimate
ultimatum

UNIT ONE

VINC/VICT
Latin VINCERE, VICTUM "to conquer"

INVINCIBLE (in vin´ sə bəl) *adj.* Unable to be conquered
L. in, "not," + vincere = *not able to be conquered*
Although the Romans thought of themselves as *invincible*, they too were eventually conquered.
syn: invulnerable   *ant:* vulnerable

PROVINCIAL (prə vin´ shəl) *adj.* Limited in knowledge of the world; narrow-minded
L. pro, "forward," + vincere = *having to do with a conquered territory*
Rory's somewhat *provincial* outlook made it difficult for her to understand what people in other parts of the world were going through.
                            ant: sophisticated

EVINCE (i vins´) *v.* To establish; to reflect the truth of
L. e, "out of," + vincere = *to overcome [as with evidence]*
The incident at the mill *evinced* the old saying, "Don't count your chickens before they hatch."

DUC/DUCT
Latin DUCERE, DUCTUM "to lead"

CONDUCIVE (kən dōō´ siv) *adj.* Supportive; encouraging; helping to bring about
L. com, "with," + ducere = *leading along with*
These noisy conditions are not *conducive* to learning or teaching.
syn: helpful, favorable

INDUCE (in dōōs´) *v.* To lead towards some action
L. in, "towards," + ducere = *lead into*
Is there any way I can *induce* you to come for coffee with me?
syn: persuade   *ant:* discourage

DEDUCE (di dōōs´) *v.* To draw a conclusion from fact; to infer
L. de, "down, away from," + ducere = *lead down from*
The detectives *deduced* from the evidence that the bank had been robbed not long before.
syn: conclude

▨ *The ancient Romans considered Rome and Italy the center of the civilized world. They thought of people living in the provinces (pro "outward," + vincere = conquered territories outside Italy) as far from civilization and unsophisticated. The word provincial still carries the idea of narrow-mindedness and lack of sophistication.*

TRACT

Latin **TRAHERE, TRACTUM** "to drag"

PROTRACTED (prō trak´ tid) *adj.* Extended in time;
   prolonged
L. pro, "forward," + tractum = *dragged forward*
There was a *protracted* struggle between the two
armies.
syn: lingering   *ant*: brief

*Though they usually broke early, PRO TRACK
stars held a PROTRACTED practice today,
running even after the sun went down.*

INTRACTABLE (in trak´ tə bəl) *adj.* Stubborn; obstinate; hard to move
   forward
L. in, "not," + tractum = *not able to be drawn forward*
Isaiah's *intractable* nature made bedtimes difficult for his mother.
syn: immovable   *ant*: malleable

RETRACT (ri trakt´) *v.* To draw back; withdraw
L. re, "back," + tractum = *to draw back*
When I found out I was wrong, I was forced to *retract* my statement.
syn: repeal

PETO

Latin **PETERE, PETITUM** "to seek aggressively, to assail, to rush"

PETULANT (pech´ ə lənt) *adj.* Irritable or short-tempered
When I told my little brother to put away his toys, he fell into a *petulant* fit and
threw the toys down the stairs.

IMPETUOUS (im pech´ ōō əs) *adj.* Acting passionately and without
   forethought
L. in, "in, towards" + petere = *rushing towards*
Because Barry was a rather *impetuous* boy, he often found himself getting into
fights over little things.
syn: rash   *ant*: careful

IMPETUS (im´ pi təs) *n.* That which drives one; momentum
L. in, "into," + petere = *rushing into*
The tragic accident at the crossroads was the *impetus* for a meeting on traffic
safety.
syn: stimulus

▩ *How do you think the
   word* petulant *evolved
   from the root* petere?

▩ *Both* impetus *and*
   impetuous *come from
   Latin* impetere, *meaning "attack."*

EXERCISES - UNIT ONE

Exercise I. Complete the sentence in a way that shows you understand the meaning of the italicized vocabulary word. *Answers will vary by student.*

1.   In order to overcome some *provincial* tendencies in my own thinking, I...

2.   The company attempted to *induce* its employees to take shorter vacations by...

3.   In one of my more *petulant* moods, I told my noisy roommate to...

4.   The army was considered *invincible* because...

5.   A *protracted* struggle over land between the two countries resulted in...

6.   It seemed rather *impetuous* of our club president to simply...

7.   Because we knew that once George made up his mind, he would be completely *intractable*, we...

8.   Many piano players find that loud noises and visual distractions are not *conducive* to...

9.   The governor decided to *retract* his statement because...

10.   Nothing *evinces* the powerful effects of pollution like...

11.   When paleontologists find a dinosaur's bones in an area, they can *deduce* that...

12.   The *impetus* for the riot that took place in the town square was most likely...

Exercise II. Fill in the blank with the best word from the choices below. One word will not be used.

   petulant   evince   invincible   protracted   retract

1.   The ____*protracted*____ debate between the two senators bored some people, but also led to some important reforms.

2.   I hardly expected a grown man to become so _____*petulant*_____ when I awakened him at three in the morning.

3.   Harry may be a good chess player, but he's not ____*invincible*____.

4.   When I realized I was wrong, I decided to _____*retract*_____ everything I had said.

Fill in the blank with the best word from the choices below. One word will not be used.

evinced   deduced   induct   conducive   impetuous

5.   When Mike saw Hugh and Lena talking and laughing together, he **deduced** that they were no longer fighting.

6.   Certain kinds of soil are more **conducive** to growing prize roses.

7.   Wasn't it kind of **impetuous** to volunteer for a job you knew nothing about?

8.   The relationship between the two characters **evinced** the main themes of the novel.

Fill in the blank with the best word from the choices below. One word will not be used.

impetus   induce   provincial   intractable   conducive

9.   After the accident with the horse, nothing could ever **induce** Albert to go back to the farm.

10.   Laughing at someone for having a different accent than yours makes you seem **provincial**.

11.   The **impetus** for his decision to play the violin was his early love of symphonic music.

12.   Jamie was so **intractable** that she refused to move her car from the sidewalk even when ordered to do so by the police.

Exercise III. Choose the set of words that best completes the sentence.

1.   The _____ argument that raged in the office for days was not _____ to getting work done.
    A. provincial; petulant
    B. impetuous; provincial
    C. petulant; protracted
    D. protracted; conducive

2.   Can we _____ from the uproar in the newspapers that the senator has refused to _____ his controversial statement?
    A. retract; induce
    B. deduce; retract
    C. evince; deduce
    D. retract; evince

3.   What was the _____ for the supposedly _____ hockey team's decision not to play in the game?
    A. conviction; induce
    B. impetus; invincible
    C. impetus; petulant
    D. provincial; retract

4. Sam became so _____ that he ran away and climbed a tree, and nothing could _____ him to come down.
    A. protracted; intractable
    B. conducive; evince
    C. petulant; induce
    D. provincial; retract

5. Nothing _____ Ben's tendency to act without thinking more than his _____ decision to become a daredevil pilot.
    A. evinces; impetuous
    B. retracts; impetuous
    C. induces; intractable
    D. deduces; provincial

Exercise IV. Complete the sentence by drawing an inference about the *italicized* word from its context.

Answers will vary by student.

1. If one boy *induces* another boy to tip over a garbage can, we can assume the second boy is...

2. If the new family in the city apartment is looked down upon for being *provincial*, they probably came from...

3. When a businessman is criticized by his boss for being *impetuous*, we can assume the businessman has probably NOT ...

Exercise V. Fill in the blank with the word from the Unit that best completes the sentence, using the root we supply as a clue. Then, answer the questions that follow the paragraphs.

Illusion or Reality?

The American mass media has an abiding interest in the paranormal. Television infomercials advertise "psychics" who convince the public that they can communicate with the dead; popular television programs pander to the public's love of occult phenomena; Hollywood produces movies that depict supernatural occurrences as factual. As billions of dollars are wasted on 900 numbers, cable subscriptions, and movie tickets, we Americans must become more critical in our acceptance of subjects and events portrayed as legitimate, from séances and ESP to UFOs and alien abductions.

What could _____*induce*_____(DUC) so many Americans to part with hundreds of dollars to learn news of the future or have some last glimpse of a departed loved one? Is it because we do not have the knowledge to protect ourselves from intellectual fraud? Surely we can exercise enough sense to stop calling hotline psychics after dozens of them have been prosecuted for criminal intent to mislead. Yet, 900 numbers exist, offering mind reading, spirit-channeling, and fortune-telling with monotonous regularity; television watchers continue to be convinced of the validity of telepathy, clairvoyance, and reincarnation.

One organization, the Committee for the Scientific Investigation of Claims of the Paranormal, believes that the mass media plays a predominant role in leading the public to accept paranormal events uncritically. If Americans were to think critically about what they were reading and viewing, says the Committee, and were also to reject the scientifically unsupported ideas about the paranormal that the media puts forth, the industry that relies so heavily on our credulity would be bankrupt.

The Committee has attempted to counter these popular media claims. In televised specials, members of the Committee carefully explain each step of an unexplainable phenomenon, such as the supposed mind-reading of a telephone clairvoyant. Even when these illusions are revealed, however, the public has a hard time accepting that sensationalism is not reality. We can _____*deduce*_____(DUC) from this reluctance that shrewd analysis of seemingly occult phenomena is less appealing than the mystique of the unknown.

Many people are troubled by the gullibility of individuals who do not take the time to investigate outrageous claims. To the mass media, however, a docile public is a reassuring constant. The general population's inability—and unwillingness—to distinguish a hoax from reality will continue to provide a(n) ___*impetus*___ (PET) for the media's focus on paranormal activity long into the future.

1. How does the writer feel about the mass media's portrayal of the paranormal?
    A. supportive of the mass media's interest in the paranormal
    B. critical of the media for portraying paranormal activity as unbelievable
    C. appreciative of the mass media for creating a nation of critical thinkers by challenging Americans to question the paranormal
    D. skeptical about both the paranormal and the media's motives in focusing on the paranormal

2. How does the Committee for the Scientific Investigation of Claims of the Paranormal try to counteract the ideas supported by the mass media?
    A. by distributing scientific material to the public
    B. by explaining the tricks behind paranormal events
    C. by producing its own television shows that reinforce the illusions of paranormal activities
    D. by releasing information about actual paranormal events

3. Why, according to the author, does the American public fail to distinguish hoaxes from reality?
    A. The media has created a nation of ready consumers.
    B. Americans cannot or will not think critically about the paranormal.
    C. The American public is constantly challenging the claims made in the movies and on television.
    D. Americans are afraid to question the media.

Exercise VI. Drawing on your knowledge of roots and words in context, read the following selection and define the *italicized* words. Note that the prefix *tra* (from *trans*) means "across," and that *e* (from *ex*) means "out from." If you cannot figure out the meaning of the words on your own, look them up in a dictionary.

Answers will vary by student.

The defense attorney attempted to win over the jury in the case by *traducing* the prosecutor's star witness. In response to the claim that his witness was a drunk, the prosecutor tried to repair the damage done with a series of questions intended to *educe* a feeling of pity for the witness from the jury. Unfortunately, after the defense's harsh attack, there was little reason for the jury to believe the witness.

UNIT TWO

FRACT/FRING/FRANG
Latin **FRANGERE, FRACTUM** "to break"

FRACTIOUS (frak´ shəs) *adj.* Tending to argue or cause discord
Malcolm grew from a *fractious* and irritable child into a tolerant and peaceful adult.
syn: cross, peevish   *ant:* amiable

INFRACTION (in frak´ shən) *n.* Minor violation of a rule or law
L. in, intensifier + fractum = *to break*
For his *infraction* of the camp code, Kevin had to peel potatoes in the kitchen.
syn: transgression

INFRINGE (in frinj´) *v.* To intrude on an area belonging to another; to
    trespass
L. in, intensifier + frangere = *to break*
Susan said her father was *infringing* upon her freedom when he took her car.

CIS
Latin **CAEDERE, CISUM** "cut, kill"

EXCISE (ik´ sīz) *v.* To cut out of; remove
L. ex, "out of," + cisum = *cut out of*
Having *excised* several paragraphs from my essay, I returned to ask my teacher's advice.
syn: expunge

INCISIVE (in sī´ siv) *adj.* Sharply cutting; direct and powerful
L. in, "into," + cisum = *cutting into*
Natasha's fast-moving narratives and *incisive* style never failed to impress us.
syn: keen   *ant:* dull

CONCISE (kən sīs´) *adj.* Brief and straightforward
L. con, "with," + cisum = *cutting with or away*
Because I had only one page to write my note on, my language had to be *concise*.
syn: terse   *ant:* rambling

▦ *A surgical* incision *is a sharp, clean cut;* incisive *thinking cuts directly to the heart of an issue.*

TOM
Greek **TEMNEIN** "to cut"

TOME (tōm) *n.* A large and serious book
G. *temnein*, "to cut"
When I removed the scholarly *tome* from the shelf, I saw that it had not been read for years.

EPITOME (i pit´ ə mē) *n.* The best or most typical example
G. epi, "upon," + temnein = *cut upon*
I hardly think I am the *epitome* of good citizenship, since I'm not even a registered voter.
syn: embodiment

DICHOTOMY (dī kot´ ə mē) *n.* Two opposite parts of one whole
G. dicho, "two," + temnein = *cut in two*
The film critic discussed the fundamental *dichotomy* in the movie.

ANATOMY (ə nat´ ə mē) *n.* The structure or parts, taken as a whole
G. ana, "up," + temnein = *cutting up (any structure)*
Maurice's *anatomy* showed the results of years of suffering.

PUNCT
Latin **PUNGERE, PUNCTUM** "to sting, pierce"

COMPUNCTION (kəm pungk´ shən) *n.* Feeling of regret or remorse
L. com, intensifier + punctum = *stinging*
Even after a long time in jail, the woman showed no *compunction* for her crime.
syn: penitence

PUNCTILIOUS (pungk til´ ē əs) *adj.* Paying strict
   attention to detail; extremely careful
Max was a *punctilious* dresser; his hat was always perfectly straight, and his shoes were always shiny.
syn: meticulous   *ant:* careless

The PUNK was PUNCTILIOUS about where to rip his jeans.

PUNGENT (pən´ jənt) *adj.* Stinging or biting, especially in taste or smell
The *pungent* aroma of garlic greeted us as we entered the restaurant.

> An epitome (literally "cut off from") was originally the book in a series that summarized the other books (think of an index to a set of encyclopedias). It now means anything or anyone who perfectly summarizes some quality.

> Whereas a puncture pierces or stings the body, compunction stings the mind.

> Just as a punctuation mark nails down a sentence, someone who is punctilious has every detail nailed down.

EXERCISES - UNIT TWO

Exercise I. Complete the sentence in a way that shows you understand the meaning of the italicized vocabulary word. *Answers will vary by student.*

1.   If the President is able to summarize the current budget problems in a *concise* way...

2.   Karen's new boss is so *punctilious* that...

3.   Once some of the material has been *excised* from the film...

4.   We could tell by its *anatomy* that the tree frog was well-suited to its surroundings because...

5.   The judge told Tim that his *infraction* of the traffic law would result in...

6.   Wei expressed her *compunction* for ruining the camera by...

7.   Richard's essay on modern American foreign policy was so *incisive* that...

8.   The author of the book sets up a *dichotomy* between...

9.   When the ruler started to *infringe* upon the rights of the citizens, people...

10. Isaac was often spoken of as the *epitome* of good manners because...

11. Darren's *fractious* behavior on the football field and in class eventually...

12. The wind blowing towards us from the landfill smelled so *pungent* that...

13. When we saw Helen leaving with the *tome*, we knew she was going to...

Exercise II. Fill in the blank with the best word from the choices below. One word will not be used.

dichotomy   infractions   tomes   punctilious   anatomy   incisive

1.   Discipline at the school is so strict that even minor **infractions** bring severe punishment.

2.   A(n) **dichotomy** certainly exists between the material world and the spiritual world.

3.   Your **incisive** wit seems to cut through all the unnecessary information and get right to the heart of the matter.

4.   The author's exhaustive writing on French history took up several weighty **tomes**.

5.   By looking at the **anatomy** of a creature, scientists can see how it has adapted.

Fill in the blank with the best word from the choices below. One word will not be used.

compunction   concise   infringe   infraction   fractious

6. If Danielle feels any ___**compunction**___ at all for lying about her homework, she should go to her teacher and apologize.

7. Carol's constant arguing and yelling made her seem so ___**fractious**___ that I wondered how anyone could stand to be around her.

8. The right to free speech is guaranteed to all Americans, and no one should ___**infringe**___ upon it.

9. A(n) ___**concise**___ summary of the day's events will be enough for me.

Fill in the blank with the best word from the choices below. One word will not be used.

excise   epitome   punctilious   anatomy   pungent

10. Cedric's friends were always telling him to loosen up and not be so ___**punctilious**___ about details.

11. Only a special kind of surgery can ___**excise**___ the tumor from the body.

12. The ___**pungent**___ scent of frying onions competed with the many other smells that filled the restaurant.

13. Grace is the ___**epitome**___ of a type of student known as "well-rounded."

Exercise III. Choose the set of words that best completes the sentence.

1. Even though Alec had committed only a minor _____ of the company rules, he was punished severely because he showed no _____.
   A. **infraction; compunction**
   B. infraction; anatomy
   C. epitome; compunction
   D. epitome; anatomy

2. Barbara is the _____ of a well-behaved child and would never _____ upon her siblings' rights.
   A. dichotomy; excise
   B. epitome; excise
   C. **epitome; infringe**
   D. dichotomy; infringe

3. For her _____ essays and _____ attention to detail, Victoria was named the best student of her English class.
   A. fractious; pungent
   B. punctilious; excise
   C. fractious; concise
   D. **incisive; punctilious**

4.   There was a definite _____ in her personality; on the one hand, she had a(n) _____
     intelligence, but on the other hand, she seemed to have no understanding of other people.
     A.   dichotomy; incisive
     B.   infraction; excise
     C.   anatomy; infringe
     D.   epitome; excise

5.   The _____ young brothers stopped their fighting and screaming when the _____
     aroma of dinner from the kitchen hit their nostrils.
     A.   incisive; concise
     B.   fractious; pungent
     C.   punctilious; fractious
     D.   pungent; incisive

Exercise IV. Complete the sentence by drawing an inference about the *italicized* word from its context.

Answers will vary by student.

1.   If a man accused of a crime hears that his new lawyer has a reputation for *incisive* thinking, he will probably feel happy because...

2.   If the doctor is going to *excise* the tumor, she will probably need instruments that can...

3.   If Dana's father walks in just as Dana is accusing Gloria of *infringing* on her privacy, he might guess that Gloria...

Exercise V. Fill in the blank with the word from the Unit that best completes the sentence, using the root we supply as a clue. Then, answer the questions that follow the paragraphs.

Exploring Ghost Sightings

Ghost sightings are one type of paranormal occurrence that has been recorded in every country throughout the world, in settings as diverse as cemeteries, subways, supermarkets, old homes, and modern, high-rise office buildings. Are these sightings indisputable evidence that spirits sometimes ___*infringe*___(FRING) upon our material world? The vast number of sightings and the numerous places where they occur convince many people of the existence of ghosts. So do the similarities of the particular elements of these sightings, elements involving all five of the human senses. People report seeing ghosts in many forms: as normal human beings with a solid ___*anatomy*___(TOM), as gauzy human figures that seem to float and appear out of a fog or a mist, or as mere spots of light moving erratically about a room. Some ghosts are not visible at all, but only make noises.

Skeptics attribute these paranormal experiences to a mixture of shadows and light, groaning and wheezing water pipes, wind, or tree branches scraping against window panes. Dedicated ghost-hunters believe, however, that the most convincing evidence involves senses other than sight and hearing, and that it is the feel, the smell, and even the taste associated with ghosts that make their supposed existence all the more difficult to dispute. For example, paranormal investigators report that a bone-chilling cold spot may spontaneously appear in a room where a ghost's presence is suspected. Special devices detect these cold spots and record the temperature. In addition to changes in the atmosphere, some visitations are accompanied by a ___*pungent*___ (PUNG) odor. Witnesses describe it as a "smell of death" and compare it to rotten eggs. Finally, some persons in the presence of a ghost experience an unexplainable metallic or sour taste in their mouths.

Tricks of the eyes and the ears, it is true, are fairly common. People are often mistaken in what they see or hear. How frequently, though, are they deceived by their senses of touch, smell, and taste? The involvement of several senses in the experience is often enough to convince a person beyond doubt that he or she has been in the presence of a ghost, despite anyone else's attempt to explain away the incident.

1.   According to the author, what senses may provide evidence that ghosts exist?
      A. sight and hearing
      B. sight and touch
      C. sight, touch, and hearing
      D. sight, hearing, touch, taste, and smell

2.   How might someone who does not believe in ghosts explain a ghost sighting, according to the essay?
      A. as the result of alcoholic consumption
      B. as the misinterpretation of visits by aliens from other planets
      C. as natural phenomena such as wind and moonlight
      D. as somebody's dream

3.   Aside from firsthand experience with ghosts, what might convince someone that ghosts exist?
      A. the tendency of skeptics to be mistaken or untruthful
      B. the similarity of ghost sightings recorded by many different people
      C. the irregular number of sightings
      D. the "smell of death"

Exercise VI. Drawing on your knowledge of roots and words in context, read the following selection and define the *italicized* words. Note that the prefix *re* means "back." If you cannot figure out the meaning of the words on your own, look them up in a dictionary.

Answers will vary by student.

Although the economy was in the beginning of a *recession*, Arthur Witherspoon was not worried about losing his job. He knew that he had worked hard, and his boss would recognize this. He arrived for work at precisely 8:00 a.m. because he believed that being *punctual* was one of his best qualities.

UNIT THREE

PEL/PULS
Latin PELLERE, PULSUM "to push, to drive"

COMPEL (kəm pel´) v. To force or strongly persuade; coerce
L. com, "along with," + pellere = *to drive along with*
The pressures of poverty *compel* many people to do things they would not do otherwise.
syn: sway

IMPULSE (im´ puls) n. A sudden, involuntary urge to do something
L. in, "within," + pulsum = *pushed from within*
When Nick saw the rows and rows of candy, he was seized by an *impulse* to spend all of his money.
syn: whim, spur

EXPEL (ik spel´) v. To send out or away
L. ex, "out of," + pellere = *to push out*
The council took a vote on whether to *expel* the treasurer for his accounting mistakes.
syn: eject   *ant*: admit

JAC/JECT
Latin JACERE, JECTUM "to throw, to cast"

CONJECTURE (kən jek´ chər) n. A guess, often one based on inadequate or faulty evidence
L. com, "together" + jectum = *thrown together*
Because you do not know where I was on the night in question, your assertions about what I did are pure *conjecture*.
syn: theory   *ant*: fact

DEJECTED (di jek´ tid) adj. Downcast or sad; depressed
L. de, "down," + jectum = *cast down*
After Mac lost the race, he sat in the corner, abandoned and *dejected*.
syn: dispirited   *ant*: animated

ABJECT (ab´ jekt) adj. Lowly, miserable and wretched
L. ab, "away," + jectum = *thrown away*
Even in the wealthiest countries, some people are forced to live in *abject* poverty.
syn: degraded   *ant*: exalted

III *Modern psychology defines* compulsive *behavior as that which a person feels forced to* act out *and powerless to stop or control. On the other hand, if a person is* impulsive, *he or she acts immediately upon urges and desires, without any thought of the consequences.*

MIT/MIS
Latin MITTERE, MISSUM "send"

EMISSARY (em´ ə ser ē) *n.* An agent sent on a
   mission
L. ex, "out," + missum = *one sent out*
During the peace talks, the young Italian
diplomat was sent as an *emissary* to Beijing.
syn: go-between

We sent out a SCARY-looking EMISSARY to speak with the enemy.

DISMISSIVE (dis mis´ iv) *adj.*   Showing little regard; scornful
L. dis, "apart, away," + missum = *sending away*
The professor responded to my confused question with a *dismissive* wave of his
hand.
syn: contemptuous

REMISS (ri mis´) *adj.* Failing to fulfill one's duty; negligent
L. re, "back," + missum = *sent back*
Do you think I was *remiss* in not cleaning up after the party?
syn: delinquent   *ant:* prudent

MOT/MOV
Latin MOVERE, MOTUS "to move"

MOTIVE (mō´ tiv) *n.* Cause for action
L. motus = *moving (reason or idea)*
The detective had the difficult job of establishing a *motive* for the murder of a
popular businessman.
syn: incentive

MOTIF (mō tēf´) *n.* A recurring theme, subject or idea
French *motif*, "dominant idea," originally from Latin *motus*
The recurring father-son *motif* in this novel makes me wonder about the author's
relationship with his own father.

EMOTE (ē mōt´) *v.* To dramatically express emotions
L. e, "out of," + motus = *to move out of (oneself)*
My sister tended to *emote* more than the other members of our shy, socially awk-
ward family.
syn: dramatize

Ⅲ Remit *means "to forgive"
or "to release from pun-
ishment." The adjective
remiss means "too forgiv-
ing, too relaxed"—i.e.,
"slack."*

EXERCISES - UNIT THREE

Exercise I. Complete the sentence in a way that shows you understand the meaning of the italicized vocabulary word. *Answers will vary by student.*

1. If the principal *expels* the students responsible for the fire, they will…

2. The sergeant sent Dan as an *emissary* to the rebel troops in order to…

3. The actor who *emotes* too much will find that the audience…

4. After she broke up with Ronnie, Francine, in an *abject* state, told her mother that…

5. When the policeman at the desk answered my questions with just a few short, *dismissive* sentences, I felt…

6. Since many of our ideas about other galaxies are nothing but *conjecture*, we should…

7. A repeated anti-war *motif* in a poem might suggest that the poet…

8. The documentary about hunger that Henry saw on television *compelled* him to…

9. A doctor would be *remiss* in his ethical responsibilities if he did not…

10. The *motive* for the theft of the football mascot's costume was probably…

11. Whenever she felt the *impulse* to run away from her problems, Mariah…

12. When Stacy was feeling *dejected*, her sister suggested she…

Exercise II. Fill in the blank with the best word from the choices below. One word will not be used.

     dismissive   motive   dejected   remiss   impulse

1. There was a heated debate over whether the cabinet official had been ___**remiss**___ in his duties when he did not report the accounting error.

2. I felt so ___**dejected**___ when I did not get admitted to the university that I did not leave my room for days.

3. Although the champion golfer was ___**dismissive**___ of his caddy's suggestions at first, he eventually gave them a try.

4. Suddenly, Henry was seized by the ___**impulse**___ to leap from the boat.

Fill in the blank with the best word from the choices below. One word will not be used.

motive   emissary   abject   motif   expel

5.   During the negotiations, the vice-president of one company was sent as a(n) ___*emissary*___ to the other company.

6.   The ___*motive*___ for the theft of the statue has not yet been determined.

7.   The baby birds, motherless and unprotected from the rain, looked ___*abject*___ and pathetic.

8.   If you ___*expel*___ the student from school for simply stating her beliefs, you will set a bad example.

Fill in the blank with the best word from the choices below. One word will not be used.

compelled   emoted   conjecture   abject   motif

9.   Some of the children in the play ___*emoted*___ too much, while others read their lines with no emotion at all.

10.   Since the critic has not read the book, anything he says about it must be considered pure ___*conjecture*___.

11.   The high winds and cold rain ___*compelled*___ us to postpone the picnic.

12.   The central ___*motif*___ of despair over lost love in the opera is introduced when the heroine takes the stage.

Exercise III. Choose the set of words that best completes the sentence.

1.   The scientific community is usually _____ of new theories at first, saying they are mere _____ instead of fact.
      A.   emotive; conjecture
      B.   dismissive; conjecture
      C.   dejected; motive
      D.   dismissive; motive

2.   The sea captain was almost overwhelmed by the _____ to abandon his ship, but he knew he would be _____ in his duties to the passengers if he did not help them.
      A.   conjecture; dismissive
      B.   motif; emotive
      C.   emissary; dejected
      D.   impulse; remiss

3. While no _____ for the theft of the money has been established, we know that the thief was living in _____ poverty and could not even afford food for his family.
  A. conjecture; abject
  B. motif; remiss
  C. motive; abject
  D. emissary; emotive

4. The _____ look on the face of our _____ to the opposing army told me he had failed to deliver his message.
  A. dismissive; conjecture
  B. emotive; emissary
  C. abject; motif
  D. dejected; emissary

5. I wanted to finish my paper on the recurring _____ I had found in the novel, but other factors _____ me to give it up.
  A. conjecture; expelled
  B. emissary; compelled
  C. motif; compelled
  D. emissary; expelled

Exercise IV. Complete the sentence by drawing an inference about the *italicized* word from its context.

Answers will vary by student.

1. If Roy learns that Sarah is *dejected*, he might call her in order to…

2. If Jeff, walking through the office, overhears Lucia say he has never been *remiss* in anything, he will probably feel…

3. If a scientist records some *conjecture* as documented fact, other scientists will probably…

Exercise V. Fill in the blank with the word from the Unit that best completes the sentence, using the root we supply as a clue. Then, answer the questions that follow the paragraphs.

A Discouraging Trend In Public Schools

If you were offered $120 to sit in a classroom for six to seven hours, and all you had to do was start and stop videotapes, would you do it? If you were offered $40,000 to take a job straight out of college that gave you two weeks of vacation at Christmas, a week for spring break, and two months off in the summer, would your first _**impulse**_ (PULS) be to jump at it? These are the opportunities awaiting substitute and certified teachers in the public schools. While the salaries offered would hardly make a person wealthy, the money is certainly not unreasonable for the level of education and preparation required. Why, then, are so many school districts experiencing teacher shortages? Why are so many college graduates _**dismissive**_ (MISS) of the opportunity to teach young minds? Why are so many veteran teachers leaving the education field, too _**dejected**_

(JECT) to prepare for another day of chaos in the halls and classrooms?

Experts point to the increasing lack of control felt by educators. Schools face the prospect of violence and mayhem unimaginable a generation ago. In recent years, the following incidents have occurred in the state of Texas alone: a former student returned to his high school, poured gasoline around a cafeteria filled with terrified students, and was about to strike a match when he was tackled by the principal; a student drew a handgun in the middle of his classroom and pointed it at his teacher; several school districts were so wracked with after-school fighting that rumors spread about a district-wide shutdown of school until tempers could ease.

The fistfights and scuffles of forty years ago and the

knife fights of twenty years ago have become the shootings of today. Some observers of this trend blame principals and teachers for being _____**remiss**_____ (MISS) in the teaching of ethical principles, while others warn that parents are too casual in monitoring their children's behavior. Whatever the beliefs, just about everyone agrees that new measures must be taken to prevent future incidents. Many districts are adopting "zero tolerance" policies for weapons on campus, installing metal detectors, and creating special police forces of their own, but will that be enough to stop the escalating violence? Or will society's priorities and values adjust again, this time making violence a less glamorous option? A generation of potential teachers—and our nation's schoolchildren—awaits an answer.

1. According to the passage, most people agree that
    A. teachers get too much vacation time.
    B. there should be "zero tolerance" for weapons on campus.
    C. teachers are paid too little.
    D. **something must be done to prevent future violence in schools.**

2. In the sentence including, "several school districts were so wracked with after-school fighting," what could be used as a *synonym* for the word "wracked"?
    A. blessed
    B. **plagued**
    C. twisted
    D. crashed

3. With which of the sentences below would the author probably agree?
    A. While school violence may seem high now, it is likely to lessen in the future.
    B. Teachers need to be less concerned with personal or financial gain and more concerned with the welfare of their students.
    C. **Unless schools deal with the cycle of violence, there will be fewer and fewer college graduates interested in teaching.**
    D. Students do not engage in fistfights any more.

Exercise VI. Drawing on your knowledge of roots and words in context, read the following selection and define the *italicized* words. Note that the prefix *inter* means "among, into," and *re* means "against, away." If you cannot figure out the meaning of the words on your own, look them up in a dictionary.

Answers will vary by student.

Mrs. Harris' classroom environment was quiet and conducive to learning. However, the tranquil setting was disturbed on Monday when Heather rudely interrupted Randy's speech on the slave trade. Before things got out of hand, Mrs. Harris *interjected* that Randy's comments were simply opinion, and that Heather's *repulsive* behavior was nothing more than the angry response of an ex-girlfriend.

UNIT FOUR

VIA
Latin **VIA** "road, way"

VIADUCT (vī´ ə dukt) *n.* A bridge that carries a road or railroad over a valley
L. via + ductum, "leading" = *road leading*
The ancient *viaduct* washed out in the heavy rains.

IMPERVIOUS (im pûr´ vē əs) *adj.* Unable to be affected
L. in, "not," + per, "through," + via = *no way through*
Andy seems *impervious* to criticism, but his feelings are very easily hurt.
syn: invulnerable

DEVIATE (dē´ vē āt) *v.* To depart, especially from a path or plan
L. de, "off, away from," + via = *off the path*
Once Rick decides on a plan for his business projects, he never *deviates* from it.
syn: stray   *ant:* continue

OBVIATE (ob´ vē āt) *v.* To make unnecessary; to avoid
L. ob, "in the way of," + via = *to get in the way*
If you take safety precautions now, you can *obviate* some future medical expenses.
syn: prevent

FER
Latin **FERRE** "to carry, to bring"

DEFER (dif ûr´) (1) *v.* To put aside until later
                     (2) *v.* To yield respectfully
L. de, "off, away," + ferre = *to put off*
(1) If Mahmoud decides to travel to France, he will have to *defer* his examinations until April.
(2) The younger doctor will *defer* to his senior partner when the patient asks a question.
syn: postpone   *ant:* hasten

DEFERENCE (def´ ər əns) *n.* Act or practice of yielding to another's authority
As new soldiers, we were warned to show *deference* to our commander in all matters.
syn: submission   *ant:* rebellion

The Romans built an elaborate system of aqueducts (literally, "water-leaders") to supply their cities and towns with water. A viaduct, rather than carrying water, carries a road over a body of water or another road.

The original meaning of obviate was to meet something that was in the way and get rid of it. Now obviate often simply means "go around" or "make unnecessary."

CONFER (kən fûr´) (1) *v.* To discuss something with someone else; consult
(2) *v.* To bestow
L. con, "together," + ferre = *to carry together*
(1) The trivia show contestant *conferred* with the other members of her team before answering the question.
(2) In a ceremony held earlier today, the government of France *conferred* several honors on the general.

INFERENCE (in´ fər əns) *n.* A conclusion not directly provided by evidence, but able to be drawn from the facts at hand
L. in, "in," + ferre = *to bring in*
When I saw the horse tracks across the snow, I made the *inference* that someone had left the gate open, allowing the horses to escape.

PROFFER (prof´ ər) *v.* To present or offer
L. pro, "forward," + ferre = *to bring forward*
When the reporter asked for more information, the policeman *proffered* a ten-page document.

ant: withhold

PROLIFERATE (prə lif´ ər āt) *v.* To increase greatly in number; multiply
L. proles, "offspring," + ferre = *to bring forth offspring*
Without natural predators, a species will *proliferate* until it overwhelms its environment.
syn: reproduce

PORT
Latin **PORTARE, PORTATUM** "to carry, to bring"

COMPORTMENT (kəm pôrt´ mənt) *n.* Manner in which one acts or behaves
L. com, "together," + portare = *bring together*
No fault could be found with my *comportment* during the awards ceremony.
syn: demeanor

PURPORTED (pər pôr´ tid) *adj.* Claimed as true, but probably false
L. pro, "forward," + portare = *brought forth*
Tim's *purported* illness kept him out of school on the day of the test.
syn: alleged   *ant*: definite

It was once PURPORTED that PORPOISES could talk.

> ⚏ Ferre is *an irregular Latin verb; one of its forms is actually latum. So any time you see "lat" in a word (dilate, relate, etc.), think of "ferre" and its meaning, "to carry."*

> ⚏ Purport *means "to claim," as in the sentence "He purports to have spoken with the President." As a noun, it means "significance," as in the sentence "The purport of the message was not clear."*

EXERCISES - UNIT FOUR

Exercise I. Complete the sentence in a way that shows you understand the meaning of the italicized vocabulary word. **Answers will vary by student.**

1. As the plants not native to this forest *proliferate* at a fast rate, the other plants will probably...

2. Although Lewis was a *purported* basketball star, we did some checking around and found that...

3. The President will *confer* with the Prime Minister in order to...

4. When Donna kept looking at her watch and tapping her foot, I made the *inference* that...

5. The judges could tell that the skater was not *impervious* to the audience's booing when the skater...

6. The orchestra showed its *deference* to the master conductor by...

7. The opening ceremonies of the library were *deferred* because...

8. You can *obviate* arguments with your friends and family by...

9. Mark's *comportment* in front of the scholarship committee will determine if...

10. Although Richard and Leah had agreed to save their money, Leah *deviated* from the plan by...

11. The army's plans for building the *viaduct* were interrupted when...

12. When the attorney *proffered* a written statement by the witness, the judge...

Exercise II. Fill in the blank with the best word from the choices below. One word will not be used.

deviate   deference   impervious   inference   obviate

1. Maddie seemed __*impervious*__ to the insults she received in the press.

2. Frank showed his __*deference*__ to his boss by allowing him to speak first.

3. The __*inference*__ you have drawn from the suspect's story is supported by new evidence we have just received.

4. If the basketball team members work on their passing, they can __*obviate*__ some of the problems they have encountered in the past.

Fill in the blank with the best word from the choices below. One word will not be used.

proliferate   impervious   defer   viaduct   purported

5. A(n) _____**purported**_____ was constructed to carry the train over the river.

6. The _____**purported**_____ prize employee was discovered loading his bag with computer equipment from the supply closet.

7. The doctors decided to _____**defer**_____ the surgery until the patient was strong enough to withstand it.

8. If the polluting corporations, already great in number, continue to _____**proliferate**_____ in this area, the eco-system could be severely damaged.

Fill in the blank with the best word from the choices below. One word will not be used.

proffered   conferred   deviate   comportment   obviate

9. When I _____**conferred**_____ with the other members of the team, I found we all had different ideas about what to do.

10. If the travelers decide to _____**deviate**_____ from their original schedule, they may add several days to the trip.

11. The tax attorney _____**proffered**_____ several documented transactions to the officials who were investigating.

12. Dr. Jones' _____**comportment**_____ in the operating room is never less than completely dignified.

Exercise III. Choose the set of words that best completes the sentence.

1. Bill's employer said that Bill's _____ was not appropriate for the situation and that he did not show _____ to his superiors.
   A. inference; viaduct
   B. comportment; deference
   C. viaduct; comportment
   D. inference; impervious

2. The candidate's advisors tried to _____ with him, but he was completely _____ to their suggestions.
   A. obviate; proliferate
   B. proliferate; purported
   C. deviate; purported
   D. confer; impervious

3. The _____ benefits of the diet disappear the minute you _____ from a strict eating plan.
    A. impervious; confer
    B. purported; deviate
    C. proliferate; obviate
    D. impervious; defer

4. Sam could not _____ his project any longer, nor could he _____ a confrontation with his teacher.
    A. defer; obviate
    B. deviate; proffer
    C. proliferate; defer
    D. confer; proffer

5. The scientists drew a(n) _____ from their data about how fast the species of waterfowl would _____ .
    A. viaduct; proliferate
    B. inference; proliferate
    C. comportment; defer
    D. deference; obviate

Exercise IV. Complete the sentence by drawing an inference about the *italicized* word from its context.

   Answers will vary by student.

1. If a forest ranger finds that a certain species of flower is not *proliferating*, he might expect that...

2. When Arnold declares that he will never *deviate* from his budget, we can infer that...

3. If the September book sale is *deferred*, it will probably take place...

Exercise V. Fill in the blank with the word from the Unit that best completes the sentence, using the root we supply as a clue. Then, answer the questions that follow the paragraphs.

Hybrids: The New Generation of Cars

"One engine is good, but two are better." So goes the new mantra of car manufacturers, and it has resulted in the growth in popularity of the hybrid automobile. With new, dual-engine systems that rely on both gas and electricity for power, hybrid cars are beginning to replace the all-gas cars of the past. Among the numerous reasons for the global trend toward a dual-powered car are a shrinking supply of petroleum, a slowly disintegrating atmosphere, and the need of a growing world population for reliable transportation. For Americans and drivers throughout the world looking to ___**obviate**___ (VIA) the effects of pollution, hybrids provide a perfect solution: they are popular, inexpensive, and virtually harmless to the environment.

Hybrid cars are not electric cars, nor are they traditional gasoline-powered automobiles. Rather, these new models combine the power of gas engines with the energy efficiency of battery engines. In this dual-engine system, electric motors are used to propel the car at low speeds and to assist the gasoline engine at higher speeds. Most hybrids also use electric motors during rests at stoplights, or when idling in heavy traffic. This innovation allows car exhaust to be substantially reduced, causing less air pollution and less noise.

The electric motors in hybrid cars run on batteries that are charged every time the car brakes. The batteries are able to store energy from braking or from the gasoline engine, much like the batteries in traditional cars do. Stored energy allows for a greater ratio of miles per gallon of gas, with hybrids able to achieve distances twice as great as gasoline-powered cars. Fuel efficiency is an important reason for the growing popularity of hybrids, as they save drivers money at the gas pump and help to reduce a growing reliance on shrinking oil reserves.

Drivers of hybrid vehicles are also doing their part to reduce the threat of global warming. The reduced use of gasoline, combined with lower emissions, has given envi-ronmentalists much to cheer about. As one driver noted, "I pay less, and my air is cleaner. Who can ask for anything more?" The recent ___*proliferate*___ (FER) of hybrid auto-mobiles on the market and on roadways seems to point towards the realization of this goal. People are driving more, spending less, and breathing easier thanks to the hybrid car.

1.   In the last paragraph, the author suggests that
     A.   the cost of electricity makes hybrid cars a more expensive means of transportation than gasoline-powered automobiles.
     B.   drivers of hybrid cars are better drivers because they have healthier lungs.
     C.   *hybrid cars are good for the environment and the wallet.*
     D.   hybrid cars are adding to the harmful effects of global warming.

2.   With which of the following statements would the author most likely agree?
     A.   Hybrid cars are economically sound, but environmentally flawed.
     B.   The reason hybrid cars are so popular is because of their futuristic look.
     C.   Traditional cars are safer for our environment because they are able to travel at faster speeds than hybrid cars.
     D.   *Hybrid cars allow motorists to decrease air pollution without sacrificing reliable and fast transportation.*

3.   Which sentence best conveys the main idea of the passage?
     A.   After years of choosing larger, less efficient cars, people now seem determined to stop wasting natural resources.
     B.   The fuel efficiency of hybrids is an important reason for the growing popularity of hybrids, as they save drivers money at the gas pump and help to reduce a growing reliance on shrinking oil reserves.
     C.   Hybrids are popular, inexpensive, and virtually harmless to the environment.
     D.   *With new, dual-engine systems that rely on both gas and electricity for power, hybrid cars are beginning to replace the all-gas cars of the past.*

4.   The purpose of the second paragraph is
     A.   to argue that gasoline-powered automobiles are slower than hybrid cars.
     B.   *to explain the main features of hybrid cars.*
     C.   to define the main similarities between gasoline and hybrid cars.
     D.   to encourage drivers to not stop at stoplights and not to slow down in heavy traffic.

Exercise VI. Drawing on your knowledge of roots and words in context, read the following selection and define the *italicized* words. Note that the prefix *de* means "away from," *col* (from con) means "together," and that *latum* (an irregular relative of *ferre*) means "carried." If you cannot figure out the meaning of the words on your own, look them up in a dictionary.

   Answers will vary by student.

Many illegal immigrants live in constant fear of *deportation*. In order to be able to remain in America, they try to find ways of earning a living that are not reported to the government. With tougher immigration laws, though, the government has made it easier to oversee the *collation* of numerous documents which help to track immigrants. The administration hopes that these new measures will lower the number of illegal aliens in America.

UNIT FIVE

VID/VIS
Latin **VIDERE, VISUM** "to see"

ENVISAGE (en viz´ ij) *v.* To imagine; to conceive of
L. in, "in," + visum = *to see into*
No matter how she tried, Larraine could not *envisage* living anywhere but California.
syn: perceive

VISAGE (viz´ ij) *n.* Face; facial expression
The twisted *visage* of the monster costume frightened the toddlers in the room.
syn: expression

PARI
Latin **PARERE, PARITUM** "be visible, appear"

APPARITION (ap ər ish´ ən) *n.* An unreal figure; a ghost
L. ad, "to," + parere = *appear to*
The first time Hamlet sees the *apparition* of his dead father, he can hardly believe his eyes.
syn: specter

SPEC
Latin **SPECERE, SPECTUM** "to look"

PERSPICACIOUS (pûr spi kā´ shəs) *adj.* Wise; insightful; acutely intelligent
L. per, "through," + specere = *seeing through*
Having praised Kate for her *perspicacious* decisions as treasurer, Nigel went on to warn her of the obstacles ahead.
syn: perceptive   *ant:* dim-witted; short-sighted

RETROSPECTIVE (re trə spek´ tiv) *adj.* Looking backward over a period of time
L. retro, "backwards," + spectum = *looking backward*
The museum will be showcasing a *retrospective* exhibit of the sculptor's works.

ASPECT (as´ pekt) *n.* A part that can be considered or viewed
L. ad, "toward," + spectum = *seen toward*
Not every *aspect* of this situation is negative; though we have made mistakes, we can learn from them.
syn: facet

INTROSPECTIVE (in trə spek´ tiv) *adj.* Contemplating one's own thoughts and
feelings
L. intro, "within," + spectum = *looking within*
The *introspective* poet enjoyed taking long walks alone.
syn: meditative   *ant*: shallow

PHAN
Greek **PHANEIN** "to appear, to show"

PHENOMENON (fə näm´ ə non) *n.* A fact or event which can be observed and/or
documented
We observed the same *phenomenon* numerous times among the songbirds.

DIAPHANOUS (dī af´ ən əs) *adj.* Lightweight and transparent
G. dia, "through," + phanein = *to show through*
The *diaphanous* curtains were lightly lifted by any breeze, no matter how slight.
syn: opaque

EPIPHANY (i pif´ ə nē) *n.* A moment of great insight;
revelation
G. epi, "near to," + phanein = *appearing near to*
The doctor's *epiphany* eventually led to a breakthrough
vaccine.

TIFFANY had an EPIPHANY while studying.

III *A Christian feast held January 6th commemorates the* Epiphany. *The events celebrated on this day all have to do with the revealing of Christ to the world.*

SYCOPHANT (si´ kə fent) *n.* A person who flatters; a yes-man
G. sukos, "fig," + phanein = *fig-displayer*
The new president of the company was surrounded by *sycophants* who never disagreed with him.

III *In ancient Athens, the law against exporting figs was not taken very seriously. Men who actually turned in fig-exporters were considered pawns of the government. From a general meaning of "pawn, subservient person," we get our meaning, "flatterer."*

EXERCISES - UNIT FIVE

Exercise I. Complete the sentence in a way that shows you understand the meaning of the italicized vocabulary word. *Answers will vary by student.*

1.   When Kaylee had an *epiphany* about a difficult math problem she had been working on, she...

2.   You can tell that Bailey is in an *introspective* mood when he...

3.   Bernard's *perspicacious* handling of his client's trial earned him a reputation as...

4.   The appearance of a comet is a *phenomenon* that can be...

5.   Because we could not tell whether the figure was a human being or an *apparition*, we...

6.   One *aspect* of the current educational system that students feel strongly about is...

7.   Debbie accused Ruben of being a *sycophant* because he...

8.   Michelle *devised* a way to solve the math problem by first...

9.   The *diaphanous* scarf falling over my thick, bulky army coat seemed...

10.   The sunken, wasted *visage* of the starved shipwreck victim made us feel...

11.   The new collection of works by the author is *retrospective*, intended to...

Exercise II. Fill in the blank with the best word from the choices below. One word will not be used.

       introspective   envisage   sycophant

1.   The city council does not ___**envisage**___ making any changes to the existing law.

2.   George was ___**introspective**___ by nature and would spend hours alone, lost in thought.

Fill in the blank with the best word from the choices below. One word will not be used.

       retrospective   diaphanous   epiphany   visage   phenomenon

3.   The exhibit takes us on a ___**retrospective**___ journey through all the films made by the director in the past thirty years.

4.   One ___**phenomenon**___ that has repeated itself is the revolt of young people against their parents' music.

5.   King William's _____*visage*_____ was peaceful in death, but also bore the lines of many years of worry.

6.   Lilah's _____*diaphanous*_____ evening dress was thought by some to be too slinky and revealing.

Fill in the blank with the best word from the choices below. One word will not be used.

     apparition   diaphanous   aspects   perspicacious   epiphany

7.   Several _____*aspects*_____ of the current financial crisis are misunderstood by the majority of the population.

8.   Was this lovely figure before me a dream, a(n) _____*apparition*_____, or a human being?

9.   Suddenly, Rachel was struck by a(n) _____*epiphany*_____ about why we lost the game.

10. Ashley believes that saving every penny is _____*perspicacious*_____, because it will protect her from hard times in the future.

Exercise III. Choose the set of words that best completes the sentence.

1.   The captain's blank _____ gave no indication that he was capable of such _____ decisions.
    A.   apparition; retrospective
    B.   sycophant; diaphanous
    C.   visage; perspicacious
    D.   phenomenon; introspective

2.   In his half-awake state, the young boy wondered if the ghostly _____ in the _____ robe was real.
    A.   phenomenon; introspective
    B.   introspective; aspect
    C.   apparition; diaphanous
    D.   perspicacious; phenomenon

3.   The geologist, working late into the night, suddenly had a(n) _____ about a(n) _____ that he had never before understood.
    A.   apparition; epiphany
    B.   phenomenon; visage
    C.   epiphany; visage
    D.   epiphany; phenomenon

4.   Even an in-depth _____ of the architect's designs could not examine every _____ of her work.
    A.   visage; apparition
    B.   retrospective; aspect
    C.   phenomenon; aspect
    D.   epiphany; visage

5.   Even in his wildest dreams, shy and _____ Darryl could not _____ his
     future as a Hollywood megastar.
     A. diaphanous; envisage
     B. epiphany; visage
     C. phenomenon; aspect
     D. introspective; envisage

Exercise IV. Complete the sentence by drawing an inference about the *italicized* word from its context.

     Answers will vary by student.

1.   If Horace makes many *perspicacious* decisions as the manager of a business, the business will probably…

2.   When one of the king's assistants is despised for being a *sycophant*, the assistant probably does things like…

3.   If Leo says that Beth should look at every *aspect* of a situation, he probably thinks that Beth should not…

Exercise V. Fill in the blank with the word from the Unit that best completes the sentence, using the root we supply as a clue. Then, answer the questions that follow the paragraphs.

Some congressmen and senators who claim they want a cleaner atmosphere also support relaxing the rules on factory emissions. Rather than reducing threats to the environment on a commercial and industrial level, they devote their attention to initiatives like the ban on public cigarette smoking. Smoking is certainly a health hazard, but it does not impose the same danger on the public as the threat of industrial emissions. Many factories have been dumping waste in lakes and streams for years, while the government closes its eyes and ears.

One example of this ___*phenomenon*___ (PHAN) occurred in New York State in the 1970s, at the site now known as Love Canal. A dumping ground for hazardous wastes was covered and used for, among other purposes, an elementary school. The chemicals that leaked out of the site caused numerous health problems among local residents, and the entire town eventually had to be abandoned. Public outrage finally made the government take a good look at Love Canal, and authorities opened an investigation into waste disposal. In response to this and other environmental disasters, the government also established the Clean Air Act, the Clean Water Act, and the Safe Drinking Water Act.

However, still trying to protect industrial progress, the government gave large firms years to implement tougher air and water purification standards. Federal and state governments should have enforced much stricter guidelines for reducing risks to the health of the general public.

The government's refusal to acknowledge pollution problems has forced many small towns to take charge of cleaning their own water without federal funding. These towns have been building plants that turn waste products into natural fertilizer, with which they cultivate their crops. Such plants must often be built and maintained with little or no help from the federal government.

This ___*aspects*___ (SPEC) of the problem should be recognized, and the government needs to allocate more funds to assist states in dealing with pollution. Moreover, authorities should insist that any factory be shut down if it refuses to control harmful emissions. As it stands, many elected representatives openly voice the need for stricter regulations, but inevitably succumb to corporate influence in exchange for campaign support. Overlooking the needs of the general population in favor of corporate interests is clearly unforgivable.

1.   What idea can you infer from the article?
      A.   People are not as important as factories.
      B.   Politicians need to make pollution a priority.
      C.   Factories are good for the environment.
      D.   A clean atmosphere is not vital to the economy.

2.   What would be the best headline for this article?
      A.   Water Pollution on the Rise
      B.   Politics Makes Strange Bedfellows
      C.   People Take Initiative for Pollution
      D.   Pollution: The Big Political Problem

3.   Small towns have taken the initiative to clean up their water supplies by
      A.   building plants to treat the sewage.
      B.   installing water faucet filters in every home.
      C.   building better sewers.
      D.   electing officials who will take an interest in clean water.

Exercise VI. Drawing on your knowledge of roots and words in context, read the following selection and
      define the *italicized* words. Note that the prefix *grandi* comes from the Latin *grandis*, meaning
      "big, great." If you cannot figure out the meaning of the words on your own, look them up in a
      dictionary.

      Answers will vary by student.

     In 1969, families across the country gathered around their television sets to watch one of the defining
moments in American history. Through the blurred lines on their screens, millions witnessed an astonishing
spectacle: members of the first crew to reach the moon hopped from their craft and began exploring the strange
surface. Astronaut Neil Armstrong, in a speech that was lofty without being *grandiloquent,* spoke the now-
famous line, "That's one small step for man, and one giant leap for mankind."

UNIT SIX

HER/HES
Latin HAERERE, HAESUM "to attach, be fixed"

ADHERENT (ad hēr´ ənt) *n.* A follower of a person or idea
L. ad, "to," + haerere = *to stick to*
Pilar was an *adherent* of the Baptist faith until about five years ago, when she converted to Catholicism.
syn: disciple   ant: opponent

INCOHERENT (in kō hēr´ ənt) *adj.* Not able to be understood; nonsensical
L. in, "not," + co, "together," + haerere = *not sticking together*
The mayor's *incoherent* speech about financial responsibility confused the audience.
syn: confused   ant: clear

INHERENT (in her´ ənt) *adj.* Existing as a natural part
L. in, "within," + haerere = *fixed from within*
In human beings, the desire to build and create is *inherent*.
syn: innate, inborn

> ▥ *You will sometimes hear glue called* adhesive. *Remember that, like adhesive, an adherent sticks to a particular philosophy or idea.*

FUS
Latin FUNDERE, FUSUM "to pour out"

DIFFUSE (di fyōōs´) (1) *adj.* not concentrated or focused; wordy
         (di fyōōz´) (2) *v.* to spread out or distribute
L. dis, "apart," + fusum = *poured apart*
(1) You can tighten up a *diffuse* essay by removing off-topic sentences.
syn: scattered   ant: concentrated
(2) The chemist noticed that the colored oil had *diffused* through the water in the glass.
syn: disperse   ant: concentrate

EFFUSIVE (if yōō´ siv) *adj.* Overflowing with words or feelings; gushing
L. ex, "out of," + fusum = *pouring forth*
The volunteers, young and *effusive*, all seemed to speak at once.
syn: enthusiastic   ant: restrained

PROFUSE (prə fyōōs´) *adj.* Plentiful; abundant
L. pro, "toward," + fusum = *pouring out (in a heap)*
The reviewers' praise for the young actor was *profuse.*
syn: bounteous

The *PROF USED PROFUSE* words to explain the workings of the solar system.

SOLU/SOLV
Latin **SOLVERE, SOLUTUM** "to loosen, to solve"

RESOLUTE (rez´ ə lōōt) *adj.* Determined; steadfast
L. re, "again," + solutum = *solving again*
The firemen faced the disaster with *resolute* courage.
syn: unshakeable

DISSOLUTE (dis´ ə lōōt) *adj.* Devoted to sensual pleasure; lacking moral restraint
L. dis, "apart," + solutum = *loosened (so as to fall apart)*
Neil's father disapproved of Neil's *dissolute,* party-centered lifestyle.
syn: dissipated; decadent

INSOLUBLE (in sol´ yə bəl) *adj.* (1) Impossible to solve or fix
(2) Unable to be dissolved
L. in, "not," + solutum + ible, "able to be" = *not able to be solved*
(1) The company's financial problems were difficult, but not *insoluble.*
syn: puzzling   *ant:* uncomplicated
(2) Because the fibers are *insoluble* in water, they take a long time to break down.
syn: tough

LEG
From Latin **LEGO, LECTUM** "to select, to choose, to gather"

DILIGENT (dil´ i jənt) *adj.* Hard-working and careful
L. dis, "apart," + legere = *setting apart; carefully selecting*
If you are *diligent* in your studies, you'll learn a lot and get good grades.
syn: assiduous   *ant:* lazy

RECOLLECT (rek ə lekt´) *v.* To remember; to recall
L. re, "again," + con, "together," + lectum = *gathered back together*
The witness could not *recollect* seeing anything unusual on the day of the crime.

SACRILEGE (sac´ rə lij) *n.* An act against a holy person or place
L. sacer, "holy," + legere = *one who collects holy objects illegally*
Many people considered the theft of the church funds not just a crime, but a *sacrilege.*
syn: profanity   *ant:* reverence

III The verb resolve *means both "to fix" and "to strongly decide." The adjective* resolute *means "strongly determined."*

EXERCISES - UNIT SIX

Exercise I. Complete the sentence in a way that shows you understand the meaning of the italicized vocabulary word. *Answers will vary by student.*

1. After Charlene finally decided that her difficulty with the car engine was *insoluble*, she...

2. Kim was such a *diligent* music student that she often...

3. In response to the *profuse* thanks of the people he had rescued, the fireman...

4. Because he is an *adherent* of a strongly anti-war religious organization, Wilson...

5. In response to the *sacrilege* committed by burglars in the temple, the rabbi ...

6. Grace's *inherent* kindness and generosity sometimes lead her to...

7. The *resolute* anger of the striking workers towards their unfair employers...

8. The actor's *effusive* acceptance speech revealed him to be a person who...

9. Percy could not *recollect* everything he had eaten for dinner because...

10. Some say the millionaire's *dissolute* habits will eventually result in...

11. Most professional speechwriters try not to be *diffuse* in their wording, because...

12. When the other board members heard the sleepy intern's *incoherent* speech, they...

Exercise II. Fill in the blank with the best word from the choices below. One word will not be used.

     resolute   inherent   diligent   incoherent   recollect

1. The witness could not _____*recollect*_____ exactly where he was on the night of the murder.

2. Although he was many times smaller than his opponent, the little dog faced the bear with ___*resolute*___ toughness.

3. Amy's dance teacher recommended her as a person who was _____*diligent*_____ enough to practice several hours each day.

4. Andrew often wondered if the desire to fight was _____*inherent*_____ in his character, since he always seemed to be arguing with someone.

Fill in the blank with the best word from the choices below. One word will not be used.

diffuse   insoluble   incoherent   inherent   sacrilege

5.   Some legal documents would be more clear if the _____*diffuse*_____ language were made concise.

6.   Do you think selling goods and services in a holy place is a(n) _____*sacrilege*_____?

7.   The medicine made Sean talk so fast he was _____*incoherent*_____; none of his friends could understand what he was saying.

8.   The birds regularly eat seemingly _____*insoluble*_____ material like tough bark and stones.

Fill in the blank with the best word from the choices below. One word will not be used.

profuse   insoluble   adherent   effusive   dissolute

9.   DJ was never a(n) _____*adherent*_____ of the "every man for himself" philosophy; he always tried to help others.

10. While one of the twins was quiet and thoughtful, the other was _____*effusive*_____ and energetic.

11. Before anyone could say that I was leading a reckless, _____*dissolute*_____ existence, I had an experience which forced me to sober up.

12. Ben expressed _____*profuse*_____ regret for hitting the fence with his car, but he still had to pay for it.

Exercise III. Choose the set of words that best completes the sentence.

1.   Though the math problem at first seemed _____ to Candace, she was _____ in working at it and eventually figured it out.
     A. eligible; incoherent
     B. dissolute; diligent
     C. profuse; eligible
     D. insoluble; diligent

2.   The first essay I ever wrote in high school was so _____ as to be _____ in places.
     A. *diffuse; incoherent*
     B. diligent; diffuse
     C. profuse; resolute
     D. inherent; diligent

3.   Cheerfulness and enthusiasm seemed to be _____ in Beverly's nature; she was _____ even when other people were more reserved.
     A. diligent; effusive
     B. dissolute; inherent
     C. *inherent; effusive*
     D. eligible; profuse

4. The detective said that the crime in the church, which many considered a(n) _____, presented a difficult, but not _____, case.
    A. adherent; insoluble
    B. adherent; diffuse
    C. sacrilege; effusive
    D. sacrilege; insoluble

5. When my teacher writes the letter of recommendation for me, I hope he will _____ how _____ I was in overcoming my learning difficulties.
    A. effusive; inherent
    B. recollect; resolute
    C. incoherent; diffuse
    D. diligent; effusive

Exercise IV. Complete the sentence by drawing an inference about the *italicized* word from its context.

   Answers will vary by student.

1. If Liza's mother scolds her for her *dissolute* behavior, we can assume her mother wants her to…

2. Katie's thank-you letters were unusually *profuse* after her birthday this year; we can therefore guess that…

3. If Rachel says Marcus was practically *incoherent* after two weeks of exams, we can infer that Marcus…

Exercise V. Fill in the blank with the word from the Unit that best completes the sentence, using the root we supply as a clue. Then, answer the questions that follow the paragraphs.

Changing Ideas on Capital Punishment

During the 1960s, support for the death penalty reached an all-time low in America. According to surveys, only 42% of Americans surveyed in 1966 were supporters of the sentence. Some opponents found it unconstitutional because of its __*inherently*__ (HER) cruelty. They believed it was a form of cruel and unusual punishment, a violation of Eighth Amendment rights. Although the Supreme Court never deemed capital punishment itself unconstitutional, widespread criticism led to the reevaluation of death penalty statutes across the country. By 1972, the Court had voided forty death penalty statutes nationwide, effectively suspending capital punishment until the states revised their guidelines.

Public support for the death penalty has increased since the 1960s, but it remains a hotly contested issue. New arguments against capital punishment focus on the apparently arbitrary imposition of the sentence and the risk of executing the innocent. Critics contend that the worst offenders do not consistently receive the death penalty. Rather, they say, the race of the defendant or victim, the quality of the defense attorneys, and the county in which the crime was committed play primary roles in determining the application of this most severe sentence.

Between 1976 and 2003, 158 African-American murder defendants were put to death. The victims in all of these cases were Caucasian. During the same period, however, only eleven Caucasians with African-American victims were executed. Critics charge that this statistic reflects the criminal justice system's tendency to value a Caucasian life more than an African-American life. Furthermore, most persons facing the death penalty must rely on public defenders for representation. The quality of such defenders has a direct impact on whether or not a person will receive the death penalty, so someone who can afford to hire a superior attorney has a better chance of avoiding a maximum sentence. Finally, it is common for a person to receive the death penalty in one state, while a person who commits a similar crime in another state is given a life sentence. All of these factors indicate the inconsistent application of the capital punishment in America.

Many people have become __*resolute*__ (SOLU) opponents of the death penalty because they believe it poses the risk of executing an innocent person. Since 1973, about ninety people on death row have been released due to the emergence of new evidence in their cases. This fact highlights the alarming possibility that some people not guilty of any crime may have been executed simply because they could not produce such new evidence.

Polls taken in 2003 report a 66% approval rate for the death penalty in America. Yet, as more people become aware of the irregularity with which the sentence is handed out, not to mention the possibility of executing innocent people, those numbers are likely to change.

1. What can you infer from the passage is the content of the Eighth Amendment?
    A. It protects the unjustly accused.
    B. It protects people from unnecessarily cruel punishment.
    C. It protects people from racial discrimination in the law.
    D. It forbids capital punishment.

2. What would be the best alternate title for this passage?
    A. Arguments Against the Death Penalty in America
    B. Supreme Court Decisions on Capital Punishment
    C. The Percentage of Americans who Support the Death Penalty
    D. How to Improve the Imposition of Capital Punishment

3. What does the author mean by the phrase "arbitrary imposition of the sentence"?
    A. The death penalty is used too frequently.
    B. The death sentence is used consistently.
    C. The death sentence is too severe a sentence.
    D. The death penalty is used irregularly.

Exercise VI. Drawing on your knowledge of roots and words in context, read the following selection and define the *italicized* words. Note that the prefix *inter* means "between, among," and the prefix *re* means "again." If you cannot figure out the meaning of the words on your own, look them up in a dictionary.

Answers will vary by student.

Out of the several dozen members who are eligible to run for office, only three have decided to do so. Julie, the first to be nominated, is a bubbly and emotional cheerleader. Hank, the second candidate, is an *intellectual* who views this election as practice for next year's presidential run for the local chapter of Brains and Looks. The last candidate, Roslyn, seems to take her campaign more seriously than others; she has *resolved* to take the office her sister lost last year.

UNIT SEVEN

FAC/FACT/FIC
Latin **FACERE, FACTUM** "to make, do"

PROFICIENT (prə fish´ ənt) *adj.* Skilled at; highly knowledgeable of
L. pro, "forward," + facere = *forward doing (going forth, achieving)*
Teresa is a *proficient* harpist, but she's also a wonderful piano player.
syn: able   *ant:* unskilled

FACTOTUM (fak tōt´ əm) *n.* An assistant who does a variety of jobs
L. facere + totum, "all, everything" = *one who does everything*
In my role as office *factotum*, I served coffee, made copies, called clients, and balanced the company checkbook.

FACSIMILE (fak sim´ ə lē) *n.* A copy or imitation
L. facere + similis, "alike" = *made alike*
The art dealer produced a *facsimile* of the painting that could hardly be distinguished from the original.
syn: reproduction   *ant:* original

FACILE (fas´ əl) *adj.* Too simplistic or easy
from L. facilis, "easy," originally from facere
The book's *facile* explanation of complex scientific principles will leave readers feeling unsatisfied.
syn: shallow   *ant:* complex

PON/POUND
Latin **PONERE, POSITUM** "to put, to place, to arrange"

EXPOUND (ik spound´) *v.* To explain or discuss in detail
L. ex, "out of," + positum = *to arrange out of*
We listened to the police chief *expound* upon the new traffic regulations.
syn: clarify

The dieter EXPOUNDED upon his EX-POUNDS.

PROPONENT (prə pō´ nənt) *n.* One who argues in favor of; supporter
L. pro, "supporting," + ponere = *to put forward with support*
Is the governor a *proponent* of stricter gun control?
syn: advocate   *ant:* critic

▥ *Both* profit *and* proficient *come from pro, "forward," +* facere.

▥ *The word* facile *has a negative connotation, but the word* facilitate *does not. Facilitate just means "to make simpler, to help along." Someone who facilitates a discussion, for instance, helps the discussion move forward.*

▥ *The* exposition *is the section of a play which explains background information, or the part of a musical piece that introduces a main theme.*

STRUCT/STRUE
Latin STRUERE, STRUCTUM "to build"

INFRASTRUCTURE (in´ frə struk chər) *n*. The basic framework of a building or a
   system
L. infra, "between," + structum = *built between*
The council discussed improvements to the *infrastructure* of the county tax program.

CONSTRUE (kən strōō´) *v*. To interpret or analyze something in a particular way
L. con, "together," + struere = *to build together (evidence)*
Alton *construed* Cindy's thoughtful silence as a rejection of his proposal.
syn: understand   *ant*: mix up

CONSTRUCTIVE (kən struk´ tiv) *adj*. Having a positive effect; helpful
L. con, "together," + structum = *to build together (to build up)*
Matt tried to provide *constructive*, but honest, advice to his coworkers.
syn: useful   *ant*: harmful

STIT/STAT
Latin STARE, STATUS "to stand"

DESTITUTE (des´ ti tōōt) *adj*. Having no money; poor
L. de, "down from," + status = *down from a standing position*
When my friends found themselves *destitute* and facing a harsh winter, they
turned to me for help.
syn: penniless   *ant*: prosperous

RESTITUTION (res tə tōō´ shən) *n*. Payment for an injury; compensation
Latin re, "again," + status = *standing again*
After Greg got food poisoning, he sued the restaurant for *restitution*.
syn: amends

STATURE (stach´ər) *n*. Level of achievement or authority; standing
L. status = *standing*
If you want to improve your *stature* in the company, try working longer hours.
syn: rank

EXERCISES - UNIT SEVEN

Exercise I. Complete the sentence in a way that shows you understand the meaning of the italicized vocabulary word. *Answers will vary by student.*

1.   Julie's *stature* in the bridge club was improved by...

2.   When I finally became *proficient* in Spanish, I was able to...

3.   Having listened to her dance teacher's *constructive* comments on posture, Nina...

4.   Jeanine was often called the family *factotum* because she...

5.   The *infrastructure* of our national banking system could be severely damaged by...

6.   After they were forced out of their apartment, the *destitute* family members...

7.   Marvin's tiny *facsimile* of the pirate ship was imperfect because...

8.   As she *expounded* upon the root causes of the Civil War, the historian...

9.   As *restitution* for the mental trauma he had endured at his workplace, Harlon received...

10. Thomas *construed* almost every situation as negative because...

11. As a *proponent* of major improvements to our public schools, Governor Marris believes that...

12. The audience reacted to the speaker's *facile* explanation of the economic problem by...

Exercise II. Fill in the blank with the best word from the choices below. One word will not be used.

proficient   restitution   infrastructure   construe   constructive

1.   The basic __*infrastructure*__ of the community may be undermined by the prolonged garbage collectors' strike.

2.   When Avram learned he was responsible for the damage to the store, he offered his services there as __*restitution*__.

3.   Until you become a __*proficient*__ marksman, you shouldn't go shooting outside the range.

4.   Many experts __*construe*__ the Prime Minister's remarks as meaning he will make changes in his economic policy.

Fill in the blank with the best word from the choices below. One word will not be used.

    facile   stature   expound   proficient

5.   Tim's essay impressed his teacher because it was complex rather than ___*facile*___.

6.   Though Maggie has not been in our club for a year, her high ___*stature*___ in our opinion has not changed.

7.   If he had an audience, Alton could ___*expound*___ for hours upon the glories of ancient Rome.

Fill in the blank with the best word from the choices below. One word will not be used.

    constructive   facsimiles   destitute   factotum   proponent

8.   The painter specializes in cheap ___*facsimiles*___ of great masterpieces.

9.   The new hockey coach insists that our comments to each other be ___*constructive*___ and positive, rather than vicious and insulting.

10.   The tornado left many members of the impoverished community completely ___*destitute*___.

11.   Although I am no ___*proponent*___ of raising taxes, I don't see any other way of obtaining money for our schools.

Exercise III. Choose the set of words that best completes the sentence.

1.   Bill is such a positive guy that even when he found himself completely _____, he did not _____ the situation as negative.
    A. proficient; expound
    B. destitute; construe
    C. proficient; construe
    D. facile; expound

2.   The speaker, a(n) _____ of expanding the national park system, began to _____ upon the need for wildlife preservation.
    A. proponent; expound
    B. stature; construe
    C. proponent; construe
    D. facsimile; expound

3. The lawsuits have gone back and forth so many times between the two parties that we must now ask whether it is _____ for either of them to demand _____.
    A. destitute; stature
    B. constructive; restitution
    C. proficient; restitution
    D. constructive; stature

4. The art critic's _____ among her peers increased when she revealed that the painting was a _____ instead of an original.
    A. proponent; infrastructure
    B. stature; restitution
    C. infrastructure; facsimile
    D. stature; facsimile

5. If the manager is _____ enough in Japanese, he can discuss the _____ of the trading plan with the businessman from Tokyo.
    A. destitute; stature
    B. proficient; infrastructure
    C. constructive; stature
    D. constructive; repose

Exercise IV. Complete the sentence by drawing an inference about the *italicized* word from its context.

   Answers will vary by student.

1. Luke is the *factotum* at the local zoo; his job probably includes…

2. When the Senator declares that he will never be a *proponent* of a law that bans smoking, journalists will probably infer that he favors…

3. When a company decides upon *restitution* in the case of an employee injured on the job, the company probably feels that…

Exercise V. Fill in the blank with the word from the Unit that best completes the sentence, using the root we supply as a clue. Then, answer the questions that follow the paragraphs.

Fairness In and Outside School

__Proponents__ (PON) of homeschoolers' exemption from standardized tests cite three main reasons for their views. Some parents feel that teachers are neglecting curriculums by focusing their attention on test preparation. Others point to studies that say standardized testing cannot accurately reflect a student's academic performance in school. Finally, there are some who claim that standardized tests may handicap students based on gender, ethnicity, or even race. While these arguments may lure some into the pro-exemption camp, the case in support of mandating testing is far more persuasive, because it is based on a student's educational and social welfare.

Students in traditional school environments are supposed to believe that standardized tests are the culmination of a year of hard work and perseverance. When home-schooled children are not required to take standardized tests, many students in traditional classroom settings __construe__ (STRUCT) their peers' exemption as meaning that school is unimportant. Tests begin to seem just another "task" without a purpose.

Lack of exposure to standardized tests places home-schooled students at a significant disadvantage. These students will eventually have to take tests for admission to college, possible job placement, and even for their drivers' licenses. By neglecting to gain proper training in test-taking techniques, as well as experience with timed test formatting, they may have a difficult time proving that they are ___*proficient*___ (FIC) in many subject areas. Standardized tests provide an assessment of an individual in relation to a community-set norm. Without taking these tests, homeschooled students are never going to know what their relationship to the community truly is.

The exemption of homeschoolers from state mandates requiring testing is reminiscent of another controversy that once existed within the educational system of this country. For decades, the idea of "separate but equal" was championed by legislators as a way of maintaining a racial separation while continuing to offer a similar education to all. As scholarship has shown, this was not an effective approach, and the level and quality of instruction between black and white schools were far from equal. In modern society, many are again championing the cause of "separate but equal," claiming that while homeschooled children and traditionally schooled children are separate, the education they receive is equal.

Without requiring mandatory testing, there is no way to prove the truth of this claim. To be truly equal, or even hint at a balance, educators need some means of comparison. Standardized test results will give them the means of such analysis.

1.   In the second paragraph, the author
     A. *discusses the impact of exemption on students' morale.*
     B. provides various theories that enhance his views on standardized testing.
     C. refutes the thesis of his essay with statistical evidence.
     D. examines segregation and discrimination within the American education system.
     E. argues that views different from his own are unproven and based on little factual information.

2.   With which of the following would the author most likely agree?
     A. Homeschooling allows students to better acquire the skills necessary for future success than traditional schooling does.
     B. *The use of college admissions exams such as the SAT and ACT favors those who are schooled in traditional environments.*
     C. The separate but equal stance maintained by legislatures during the civil rights era was justified and should be continued today.
     D. Standardized exams allow students to show their inner qualities and the traits that make them unique in society.

3.   The author's point in writing this essay is
     A. to inform readers of the difference between traditional schooling and homeschooling.
     B. to prove that standardized test scores are good indications of homeschooling success.
     C. to argue that homeschoolers should not be required to take standardized tests.
     D. *to argue that homeschoolers should be required to take standardized tests.*

Exercise VI. Drawing on your knowledge of roots and words in context, read the following selection and define the *italicized* words. Note that *pre* means "before," and *de* means "down from." If you cannot figure out the meaning of the words on your own, look them up in a dictionary.

Answers will vary by student.

Author Jack Proutt begins his book on <u>Moby Dick</u> with a *preface* that offers readers the opportunity to learn the history of the novel. In the chapters that follow, Proutt uses *deconstructive* literary theory to break down the novel into its essential elements in order to gain a better understanding of the work. Critics are hailing the work as "groundbreaking," "a literary gem," and as "the most important study of Melville to hit shelves in decades."

UNIT EIGHT

PLAC
Latin **PLACERE, PLACITUM** "to please"

COMPLACENT (kəm plā´ sənt) *adj.* Satisfied with a situation that should be
    changed or improved
L. com, intensifier, + placere = *too pleased*
Susanna saw that the children were becoming lazy and *complacent,* so she urged
them to become involved in volunteer work.
syn: smug

PLACEBO (plə sē´ bō) *n.* Something which has a positive mental effect, but no
    physical effect
L. literally, "I will please"
Good news on the political front is often a *placebo* for the stock market, even if it
becomes bad news again the next day.
syn: quick fix

PLACID (plas´ id) *adj.* Calm; undisturbed
Tara's *placid* expression never seemed to register the chaos around her.
syn: peaceful   *ant:* agitated

GRAT
Latin **GRATUS** "pleasing, earning thanks" or "thankful"

GRATUITOUS (grə tōō´ i təs) *adj.* Unnecessary or unwanted
L. gratus   *done only to please (unasked for, unneeded)*
Movies today are often criticized for *gratuitous* violence.
syn: unessential   *ant:* important

INGRATIATE (in grā´ shē āt) *v.* To gain another's favor by flattery or false
    friendliness
L. in, "in, to" + gratus = *into favor*
Annie suspected that the student was trying to *ingratiate* himself with his
teachers.

INGRATE (in´ grāt) *n.* One who is not properly thankful
L. in, "not," + gratus = *not thankful*
When Amber threw down her birthday present in disappointment, she seemed a
spoiled little *ingrate.*

---

*⫿ To test the effective-
ness of a new medicine,
a doctor may give one
group of patients a pla-
cebo (sometimes called
a "sugar pill"). It has no
actual healing powers, but
provides a control against
which to test the group
actually taking the medi-
cine.*

*⫿ A tip is sometimes
called a gratuity; it is
not required, but a person
grateful for a service may
leave one.*

DOC/DOCT
Latin **DOCERE, DOCTUM** "to teach"

DOCILE (dos´ əl) *adj.* Easily taught; submissive to instruction
L. docilis = *able to be taught*
Ruffles, who had previously been the most *docile* of the cats, suddenly started hissing and biting.
syn: obedient   *ant:* defiant

INDOCTRINATE (in dok´ tri nāt) *v.* To teach a certain point of view to
L. in, "into," + docere = *to teach into*
The cult leader attempted to *indoctrinate* his new followers in the ways of his teachings.
syn: instill

DOCTRINE (dok´ trin) *n.* That which is taught; body of beliefs or ideas
L. doctrina = *a teaching*
Followers of this political *doctrine* believe that war is the solution to most political problems.
syn: creed

⫦ *Other synonyms for* docile *are* meek, mild, *and* gentle. *Other antonyms include* stubborn, mean, *and* vicious.

TEMPER
Latin **TEMPERARE, TEMPERATUM** "to temper, make less severe"

TEMPER (tem´ pər) *v.* To decrease the strength of
Serita *tempers* her spicy stew with a little milk or yogurt.

TEMPERANCE (tem´ pər ens) *n.* Restraint or moderation, especially in regards to alcohol or food.
Jordan's *temperance* at the buffet table spared her the indigestion that I got.
syn: frugality   *ant:* indulgence

For many, the TEMPLE was a place of TEMPERANCE.

⫦ *Be careful not to mix up the* temper *and* tempor *roots. If you see* tempor *(as in the word* temporal*), look for a meaning having to do with time.*

INTEMPERATE (in tem´ pə rit) *adj.* Lacking moderation; severe or extreme
L. in, "not," + temperatum = *not tempered*
In terms of climate, the Sahara desert and Antartica are two of the most *intemperate* places in the world.
syn: rigorous

EXERCISES - UNIT EIGHT

Exercise I. Complete the sentence in a way that shows you understand the meaning of the italicized vocabulary word. *Answers will vary by student.*

1.   Annie was critical of Ramon's political *doctrine* because…

2.   Harry's attempt to *ingratiate* himself with Nina actually resulted in…

3.   Because I exercised *temperance* when the first round of food and drink was served…

4.   The *docile* mare allowed herself to be led into the stable without…

5.   Before you become *complacent* about your financial situation…

6.   If Lloyd *tempers* his constant stream of criticism with a few positive remarks, he will find that…

7.   Although she appeared to be rather *placid* in nature, Dora…

8.   The winning lottery ticket was a *placebo* for the whole town's problems, in that it…

9.   Some of the *gratuitous* luxuries in the hotel suite included…

10.   After his journey to the *intemperate* land of North Dakota, Mel swore…

11.   The coach tried to *indoctrinate* his players with his philosophy of baseball by…

12.   Some people called the striking workers *ingrates*, but others said that…

Exercise II. Fill in the blank with the best word from the choices below. One word will not be used.

docile   complacent   tempered   placebo   ingratiate

1.   My ___*docile*___, good-natured little brother is a favorite of his teachers.

2.   Rather than trying to ___*ingratiate*___ herself with her new coworkers, Maxine earned their respect by doing excellent work.

3.   Lester was just beginning to grow ___*complacent*___ about his grades when he encountered the most difficult math test he had ever seen.

4.   Although many children find the first day of school scary, their nervousness is ___*tempered*___ by the excitement of new people, sights, and sounds.

Fill in the blank with the best word from the choices below. One word will not be used.

      gratuitous   doctrine   placebo   placid   indoctrinate

5.   Awarding an "A" in math to everyone would only be a(n) ___*placebo*___ for the students; it wouldn't lead to real academic improvement.

6.   Penny didn't follow a particular religious ___*doctrine*___ because she couldn't decide which one was right.

7.   Since he had no opponent in the election, the candidate's campaign ads seemed rather ___*gratuitous*___.

8.   If the political party cannot ___*indoctrinate*___ its youngest members with its core values, how will it win the election?

Fill in the blank with the best word from the choices below. One word will not be used.

      docile   ingrate   placid   temperance   intemperate

9.   I was amazed at the ___*temperance*___ Theo showed when faced with all kinds of temptations.

10.   Mary didn't want to seem like a(n) ___*ingrate*___, so she graciously thanked her aunt for the sweater.

11.   The ___*placid*___ expression of the moose as it stared into the window was very different from the hysterical expression of the human staring back.

12.   The ___*intemperate*___ conditions on the top of the mountain made it difficult for anyone to survive.

Exercise III. Choose the set of words that best completes the sentence.

1.   Roberta's fiery nature was _____ by her best friend's _____ character.
    A. ingratiated; gratuitous
    B. indoctrinated; complacent
    C. tempered; docile
    D. indoctrinated; docile

2.   Darryl found that _____ luxuries tended to make him _____.
    A. intemperate; placid
    B. gratuitous; complacent
    C. placid; docile
    D. docile; complacent

3.   In a naturally _____ climate, sunshine seems almost to be a(n) _____; it briefly makes everyone feel better, even though it doesn't last.
    A. placid; temperance
    B. complacent; ingrate
    C. gratuitous; ingrate
    D. intemperate; placebo

4. While one of the sisters was too _____ and would not argue even when she should have, the other was a(n) _____ who was never satisfied with any gift or kind word.
    A. gratuitous; placebo
    B. *placid; ingrate*
    C. complacent; intemperate
    D. intemperate; temperance

5. The _____ that Emma follows is so strict that she has to _____ the severity with amusement once in a while.
    A. temper; ingrates
    B. *doctrine; temper*
    C. placebo; ingratiate
    D. temperance; indoctrinate

Exercise IV. Complete the sentence by drawing an inference about the *italicized* word from its context.

Answers will vary by student.

1. If an outside visitor to the company sees Frank trying to *ingratiate* himself with Mr. Leavis, he might assume that Frank wants...

2. If Doreen complains about the *intemperate* climate of the place she visited last year, Nancy can assume Doreen did not...

3. If Isaac knows that Pinky is the most *docile* rabbit in the petting zoo, he might expect the children who visit to...

Exercise V. Fill in the blank with the word from the Unit that best completes the sentence, using the root we supply as a clue. Then, answer the questions that follow the paragraphs.

The Reality of Reality TV

Many modern media critics argue that television viewers have become increasingly __*complacent*__ (PLAC) in accepting reality programs. Others deplore network executives' attempt to __*ingratiate*__ (GRAT) themselves with viewers by presenting senseless spectacles and low-class programming. Serious dramas and lighthearted sitcoms are being shelved due to increasing costs, lack of innovation, and an inability to draw viewers away from an ever-expanding number of cable stations. To understand why reality programs have infiltrated the airwaves, however, it is important to look at the demise of traditional television programming.

Since television began, programming and costs have been its driving factors. One theory as to why this is the case states that, in order to gain a larger audience, networks must pay attention to what people want to watch. Popular programming, according to this line of thinking, attracts larger audiences, and larger audiences mean increased revenues from advertising. Television executives, therefore, need to understand that they must sell an audience what it wants, but they have been slow to do so. The networks' competition, cable, has learned this concept more rapidly than the networks themselves have.

With the advent and growth of cable television, the once-limited spectrum of channels has become a never-ending banquet of __*gratuitous*__ (GRAT) viewing possibilities. From music networks to food channels, news to sports, family-centered programming to television for animal-lovers, it seems that today, there are channels for everyone, no matter how small the audience. With the increased number of networks, though, come more competitors for the same number of viewers. This competition invariably leads to smaller budgets for the programs themselves. Looking to ease the pain caused by tightened budgets, cable and network programmers quickly realized that reality television shows were a means of providing a cheap and popular alternative to traditional programming.

As long as viewers flock to these new programs,

both networks and cable will continue to produce them in countless numbers. The low production costs, large audiences, and rapid development of reality-based shows allow the networks to adhere to one of the fundamental ____*doctrines*____ (DOCT) of the industry: regardless of what is good for the viewers, television will always seek to maximize its audience while minimizing its cost.

1. The main purpose of the essay is
    A. to explain why reality programming has become so common on network television.
    B. to further the author's idea that reality programming is superior to traditional television shows.
    C. to explain the production process of reality programming.
    D. to argue that cable television is going to take over traditional network television.

2. Which of the following is the best summary of this essay?
    A. Serious dramas and lighthearted sitcoms are being shelved for their increasing costs, lack of innovation, and inability to draw viewers away from cable stations.
    B. Critics are giving viewers senseless spectacles and low-class programming.
    C. Television programming has always been a balancing act between what television viewers want and what advertisers will pay for.
    D. To understand why reality programs have infiltrated the airwaves, however, it is important to look at the demise of traditional programming.

3. The author's tone in assessing the demise of traditional programming is best described as
    A. informative.
    B. gratuitous.
    C. docile.
    D. intemperate.

Exercise VI. Drawing on your knowledge of roots and words in context, read the following selection and define the *italicized* words. If you cannot figure out the meaning of the words on your own, look them up in a dictionary.

Answers will vary by student.

The new chef at Pancake House tried hard to *placate* her sometimes demanding customers. She spent several hours preparing foods that would appeal to eaters young and old. She has been quoted as saying, "The most *gratifying* aspect of being a chef is watching people smile after a meal." Judging from the smiles on Pancake House diners, Chef Elizabeth has much to be pleased about.

UNIT NINE

TORT/TORQ
Latin **TORQUERE, TORTUS** "to twist"

TORTUOUS (tôr ´ chōō əs) *adj.*   Not direct or straightforward
L. tortus = *twisting*
The *tortuous* road up the mountain was difficult and dangerous to navigate in the dark.
syn: circuitous   *ant:* straightforward

RETORT (ri tôrt´) *v.* To respond critically or sarcastically
L. re, "back," + tortus = *to twist (words) back*
When I complained that Paula had given me bad directions, she *retorted* that I should have looked at a map.
syn: reply

EXTORT (ik stôrt´) *v.* To wrongly or illegally force someone to comply with a
     demand
L. ex, "out of," + tortus = *twisted out of*
Because the corrupt official possessed potentially damaging information about his colleagues, he wanted to *extort* money from them.
syn: coerce   *ant:* coax

VOLV/VOLU
Latin **VOLVERE, VOLUTUM** "to roll, to turn"

VOLUBLE (vol´ yə bəl) *adj.* Talkative; given to rapid, abundant speech
L. volutum = *rolling out (words)*
Our new recruit was an enthusiastic and *voluble* young man who would strike up a conversation with anyone.
syn: chatty   *ant:* quiet

CONVOLUTED (kän´ və lōō´ tid) *adj.* Having too many twists and turns; overly
     complicated
L. con, "together," + volutum = *to roll together*
Sarah looked skeptical when she heard my *convoluted* excuse for being late.
syn: tangled   *ant:* clear

EVOLVE (ē volv´) *v.* To unfold; to develop or change gradually
L. e, "out of," + volvere = *to turn out*
Our volunteer group started out small, but *evolved* into a large, statewide organization.
syn: progress   *ant:* regress

> ⛉ Torturous *means "like or relating to torture," while* tortuous *means "winding" or "twisting."*

> ⛉ Extortion *usually involves some secret threat to a person's property or reputation. Blackmail is an example of extortion.*

> ⛉ *Whereas evolution is slow and gradual change,* revolution, *meaning "a sudden turning over," is sudden, often violent, change.*

FLEX/FLECT
Latin **FLECTERE, FLECTUM** "to bend"

INFLEXIBLE (in flek´ sə bəl) *adj.* Too unchangeable in character or purpose
L. in "not," + flectum = *not bending*
Some of Greg's students thought of him as an *inflexible* tyrant because he never
allowed them extra time for assignments.
syn: rigid, stiff   *ant*: flexible

DEFLECT (dē flekt´) *v.* To cause to turn aside or away
L. de, "away," + flectum = *turn (something) aside*
Joe skillfully *deflected* his opponent's blows with an upraised arm.
syn: redirect   *ant*: accept

INFLECTION (in flek´ shən) *n.* Change in pitch or tone of the voice
L. in, "in," + flectere = *to bend (the voice)*
If you want to make your meaning clearer, try a different *inflection* on the first
words of the poem.

A tonsil INFECTION changed the
singer's INFLECTION.

VERT/VERS
Latin **VERTERE, VERSUM** "to turn"

ADVERSE (ad vûrs´) *adj.* Not helpful; harmful
L. ad, "against," + versum = *turned against*
We were pleased to have made it up the mountain under such *adverse* conditions.
syn: unfortunate, injurious   *ant*: conducive

REVERT (ri vûrt´) *v.* To fall back into an old condition
Latin re, "back," + vertere = *to turn (something) back*
Annie hopes never to *revert* to the bad habits she gave up.
syn: lapse   *ant*: improve

SUBVERT (səb vûrt´) *v.* To undermine; to corrupt
Latin sub, "beneath," + vertere = *to turn from beneath*
The queen was afraid the rebellious subjects would *subvert* her authority.
syn: invalidate   *ant*: support

▥ *Have you ever heard
someone mention genu-
flecting before a holy
figure or royal person? To
genuflect is to "bend at
the knee."*

EXERCISES - UNIT NINE

Exercise I. Complete the sentence in a way that shows you understand the meaning of the italicized vocabulary word. **_Answers will vary by student._**

1. It was clear that the author's poems *evolved* because…

2. In an attempt to *extort* money from the businessmen in his district, the councilman…

3. The manager who was caught stealing from the company tried to *deflect* criticism of himself by…

4. When the rebel leader tried to *subvert* the authority of the military government,…

5. The author employed some peculiar *inflections* while reading the poem, leading the audience to…

6. When the interviewer accused the singer of being a drama queen, the singer *retorted* that…

7. Some of the *adverse* circumstances facing the young violinist were…

8. During the *tortuous* journey along the winding, overgrown mountain path…

9. Although known as an *inflexible* interpreter of the Constitution, the Supreme Court Justice…

10. I found the film's central plot so *convoluted* and difficult to follow that…

11. The book salesman standing on our front porch was so *voluble* that…

12. Sharon *reverted* to some of her old patterns of eating because…

Exercise II. Fill in the blank with the best word from the choices below. One word will not be used.

     revert   voluble   adverse   extort   evolve

1. With the help of my friends, I not only got through a(n) ___**adverse**___ situation, but I also learned from it.

2. When the new computer system crashed because of a virus, we had to temporarily ___**revert**___ to an old one.

3. Rather than using the appropriate legal channels, Sid tried to ___**extort**___ information from members of the city council.

4. One of the more ___**voluble**___ teachers kept talking even after the bell rang, and his students were forced to stay and listen.

Fill in the blank with the best word from the choices below. One word will not be used.

      deflected   inflexible   evolve   retort   tortuous

5.   The audience had the pleasure of watching a good opera _____*evolve*_____ into a truly spectacular one.

6.   I try to be open-minded rather than _____*inflexible*_____ when it comes to the subject of love.

7.   A quick, sarcastic _____*retort*_____ silenced the journalist who had asked an inappropriate question.

8.   Our small, agile boat could easily navigate the _____*tortuous*_____ curves of the river.

Fill in the blank with the best word from the choices below. One word will not be used.

      deflect   adverse   inflection   convoluted   subvert

9.   By varying the _____*inflection*_____ on a particular word or note, a singer can bring many different meanings out of the same song.

10.   The reasoning behind the budget disaster was so _____*convoluted*_____ that no one could begin to untangle it.

11.   In an attempt to _____*subvert*_____ the election results, the crooked politician threw away several boxes of ballots.

12.   You will not always be able to _____*deflect*_____ criticism away from yourself.

Exercise III. Choose the set of words that best completes the sentence.

1.   When you find yourself facing _____ circumstances, will you be able to adapt, or will you be _____?
    A. convoluted; tortuous
    B. adverse; voluble
    C. adverse; inflexible
    D. inflexible; convoluted

2.   On some days Nicki felt she was _____ into a mature, graceful person, but on others she _____ to her old, bad habits.
    A. evolving; deflected
    B. deflecting; subverted
    C. evolving; reverted
    D. extorting; evolved

3.   In an attempt to _____ the power of the ruling party, the corrupt official tried to _____
     money from the vice president.
     A. retort; revert
     B. devolve; retort
     C. subvert; extort
     D. retort; devolve

4.   I could barely stand to listen to Kim recite the poem; almost every _____ seemed wrong to me,
     and I found the poem _____ and confusing anyway.
     A. inflection; inflexible
     B. retort; voluble
     C. inflection; convoluted
     D. retort; adverse

5.   When I teased Marge for being stern and _____, her _____ was that I would go along
     with anyone.
     A. tortuous; inflection
     B. adverse; retort
     C. voluble; inflection
     D. inflexible; retort

Exercise IV. Complete the sentence by drawing an inference about the *italicized* word from its context.

Answers will vary by student.

1.   If a group of citizens tries to *subvert* the influence of a large corporation, the citizens probably feel that
     the corporation…

2.   If Larry says that Carl tried to *extort* information from him, we can assume that Larry…

3.   If Kathy says that she has *reverted* to her smoking habit in the month of December, in November she
     probably…

**Exercise V. Fill in the blank with the word from the Unit that best completes the sentence, using the
     root we supply as a clue. Then, answer the questions that follow the paragraphs.**

The Perseverance of Thomas Edison

"Just because something doesn't do what you planned it to do in the first place doesn't mean it's useless… Surprises and reverses should be an incentive to great accomplishment." This quote from Thomas Alva Edison applies nicely to his own life and work. Had he been more **inflexible** (FLEX), he could never have adjusted to the countless instances of rejection that preceded his enormous and important successes. Edison's determination to adapt to anything he deemed a challenge profited the world in ways few people could imagine at the time.

Edison's fierce resolve developed partly in reaction to **adverse** (VERS) circumstances. At age fourteen, he contracted scarlet fever, which robbed him of all the hear-ing in his left ear and 80 percent in the right. For the rest of his life, he would be driven to understand and solve the problems people face in dealing with their environments. Fortunately, he had enough foresight to understand the importance of the whole problem-solving process. "If I find 10,000 ways something won't work, I haven't failed," he said. "I am not discouraged, because every wrong attempt discarded is just one more step forward."

As he became an adult, Edison's youthful optimism **evolved** (VOLV) into a powerful drive to succeed. During the quiet hours of his job at Western Union, he worked feverishly on an electronic voting machine and applied for his first patent. The Massachusetts Legislature rejected the invention, leaving him with a beautifully designed machine that could not be marketed. Consequently, Edison vowed to "never waste time inventing things that people would not want to buy." However, this vow did not stop him from conducting experiments that were not certain to succeed. He viewed his 500 to 600 abandoned patent applications as homework.

In 1869, a corporation paid Edison $40,000 for the rights to his stock-ticker, which set him on a trail of creating successful inventions for industrial use. At age 29, he invented the carbon transmitter, which ultimately led to devices like the telephone and the phonograph. The first incandescent electric light bulb, a centrally generating and distributing electric power system, and the first silent motion picture soon followed. By the 1920s, Edison was producing defensive devices for submarines and ships and many other useful inventions related to rubber, concrete, and ethanol. Edison eventually patented over 1,000 inventions in his desire to benefit mankind.

"I never perfected an invention that I did not think about in terms of the service it might give others," he once said. "I find out what the world needs, then I proceed to invent." Without Edison's perseverance and spirit of service, many advances in technology would never have been possible.

1. What did Edison mean when he said, "If I find 10,000 ways something won't work, I haven't failed"?
    A. Failure in an experiment can be a kind of success.
    B. Failures come when something will not work.
    C. Success is profit.
    D. Success comes only when something will not work.

2. According to the passage, which of the following would Edison probably consider a failure?
    A. a rejected patent application
    B. lack of education
    C. giving up on an invention
    D. a financial disaster

3. Edison believed that inventions could always be improved, and ideas could always
    A. evolve.
    B. deflect.
    C. extort.
    D. subvert.

Exercise VI. Drawing on your knowledge of roots and words in context, read the following selection and define the *italicized* words. Note that the prefix *in* means "not." If you cannot figure out the meaning of the words on your own, look them up in a dictionary.

Answers will vary by student.

The *voluminous* works of famous author Charles Dickens fill an entire bookshelf. The countless novels, short stories, and other writings have kept literary scholars busy for years studying the Victorian themes that Dickens explored. One scholar, Harvey Forrester, was lucky enough to *inadvertently* find a connection between Dickens and one of his most famous characters–Oliver Twist. Forrester noticed that Dickens and Twist both shared a passion for travel and adventure. For Forrester, the find was career-defining.

UNIT TEN

CRIMIN

Latin **CRIMEN** "crime, charge of crime"

DECRIMINALIZE (dē krim´ ən əl īz) *v.* To do away with legal penalties for
L. de, "away, off," + crimen = *(to take) a crime away*
Eric is part of a group that is calling upon the government to *decriminalize* certain drugs.

INCRIMINATE (in krim´ ə nāt) *v.* To reveal guilt or make (someone) appear
   guilty
L. in, "onto," + crimen = *(put) crime onto*
If the stolen necklace we found in your drawer doesn't *incriminate* you, I don't know what does.
syn: implicate   *ant:* acquit

RECRIMINATION (rē krim´ ə nā shən) *n.* An accusation made in reply; a counter-
   charge
L. re, "back," + crimen = *charge (made) back*
The two friends got into a bitter fight and began hurling *recriminations* at one another.
syn: rebuke

CULP

Latin **CULPARE, CULPATUM** "to blame"

CULPABLE (kul´ pə bəl) *adj.* Deserving blame
L. culpatum + able = *able to be blamed*
Marshall, who ran the Tilt-a-Whirl, considered himself *culpable* for the accident at the amusement park.
syn: liable   *ant:* blameless

CULPRIT (kul´ prit) *n.* One responsible for a crime
Police currently have no idea who the *culprit* behind the fire might be, but they have a long list of suspects.
syn: perpetrator

MEA CULPA (mā´ ə kul´ pə) *interjection* Statement uttered to show personal
   responsibility for a wrong
Directly from Latin *mea culpa*, "my fault"
"*Mea culpa!*" said Miguela, with some embarrassment, when she realized that she'd left the car windows down.

ONUS/ONER
Latin ONUS "burden"

ONUS (ō′ nəs) *n.* Burden or obligation
The *onus* of proving that this man was at the crime scene now rests on the detective.
syn: duty

ONEROUS (on′ ər əs) *adj.* Unpleasant and burdensome
Dr. Lassiter faced the *onerous* task of telling the patient that his cancer had spread.
syn: demanding   *ant:* easy

Since nobody else would do it, the ONUS of moving the piano was ON US.

EXONERATE (ig zon′ ə rāt) *v.* To prove not guilty
L. ex, "out of," + onus = *out of the burden (of proof)*
We feel sure the evidence we have uncovered will *exonerate* Anna.
syn: acquit   *ant:* condemn, convict

Ⅲ Onus *is usually used in legal settings; the onus probandi, or "burden of proof," is that which a person must convince a judge or jury to believe.*

PROB/PROV
Latin PROBARE, PROBATUM "prove good, approve"

APPROBATION (ap rə bā′ shən) *n.* Praise or approval
L. ad, "towards," + probare = *to take approval towards*
Ellen won widespread *approbation* for her work in biomedical research.
syn: commendation   *ant:* condemnation

REPROBATE (rep′ rə bāt) *n.* A dishonest or immoral person; a scoundrel
L. re, "back, away from," + probare = *one away from approval*
The *reprobates* who set fire to the forest must be caught and punished.
syn: delinquent

REPROVE (ri prōōv′) *v.* To scold or criticize
L. re, "back," + probare = *approval back*
My aunt Thelma gently *reproved* me for taking more than my share of dessert.
syn: chide   *ant:* praise

Ⅲ *The Latin* probare *means "to test" and "to test something for goodness." We get both* prove *and* approve *from this verb.*

EXERCISES - UNIT TEN

Exercise I. Complete the sentence in a way that shows you understand the meaning of the italicized vocabulary word. *Answers will vary by student.*

1. When Jed called out *"Mea culpa!"* in response to the malfunction of the copier, we knew that…

2. The police will catch the *culprit* behind the wave of vandalism by…

3. The other members of the political party showed their *approbation* of the idea by…

4. Even though all the evidence seems to *incriminate* Mr. Dawson,…

5. When I was younger, I had a reputation for being somewhat of a *reprobate* because…

6. Rather than *exonerating* the driver of the car, the footage from the traffic camera…

7. One crime that really doesn't harm anyone and should therefore be *decriminalized* is…

8. When Ray *reproved* Caroline for leaving the toys on the stairs, she…

9. The most *onerous* job a farmer of today has to do is probably…

10. Because I consider myself *culpable* for the boat accident, I will…

11. The *onus* of proving that a dog is not dangerous should be borne by…

12. As the two men exchanged *recriminations*, their friends…

Exercise II. Fill in the blank with the best word from the choices below. One word will not be used.

exonerate   reproved   culprit   onerous   approbation

1. When Josie's mother __*reproved*__ her for coming home late, Josie hung her head in shame.

2. I was given the __*onerous*__ job of dealing with a huge crowd of impatient and complaining customers.

3. The __*culprit*__ in the cookie theft is probably between three and six years old.

4. Do the defendant's lawyers hope the new testimony will __*exonerate*__ their client?

Fill in the blank with the best word from the choices below. One word will not be used.

> reprove   recriminations   reprobates   approbation   decriminalize

5. Some people argue that we should __*decriminalize*__ speeding, but others think we should make the laws tougher.

6. The principal felt that the boys were habitual __*reprobates*__ and should be expelled from school.

7. Jesse refused to state publicly what __*recriminations*__ he had included in the angry letter to his boss.

8. The __*approbation*__ of the judges' panel meant a lot to the nervous young dancer.

Fill in the blank with the best word from the choices below. One word will not be used.

> onus   incriminated   mea culpa   culpable   reprobate

9. Just being present when an accident occurs doesn't make you __*culpable*__ for that accident.

10. Philip now carries the __*onus*__ of defending his brother's good character.

11. My father said that my guilty expression __*incriminated*__ me more than anything else.

12. When I saw that my actions had caused a fight between my friends, I thought to myself, "__*mea culpa*__."

Exercise III. Choose the set of words that best completes the sentence.

1. The young man accused of the crime may have a reputation for being a(n) _____, but reputation alone is not enough to _____ him.
    A. onerous; decriminalize
    B. reprobate; incriminate
    C. onus; reprove
    D. culprit; decriminalize

2. By expressing _____ when you should _____, you are sending a message that bad behavior is acceptable.
    A. recrimination; incriminate
    B. approbation; decriminalize
    C. approbation; reprove
    D. onus; incriminate

3. The _____ of proving that the man is not the _____ who committed the crime falls on his team of lawyers.
    A. onus; culprit
    B. onus; approbation
    C. culprit; recrimination
    D. culprit; onus

4. If the city council should choose to _____ speeding, they would be _____ for any injury received as a result of speeding.
    A. exculpate; onerous
    B. decriminalize; culpable
    C. incriminate; reprobate
    D. exonerate; onerous

5. Patrick felt that if he could _____ Francine of the charge against her, he would earn her _____ and respect.
    A. exonerate; approbation
    B. incriminate; culprit
    C. reprove; reprobate
    D. reprove; approbation

Exercise IV. Complete the sentence by drawing an inference about the *italicized* word from its context.

    Answers will vary by student.

1. If someone passing by a rally notices that a speaker has earned the *approbation* of his listeners, the passerby might assume…

2. If a voter who knows nothing about two political figures hears them trading *recriminations*, the voter might guess the two figures are…

3. When an investigation concludes that one driver in a two-car wreck is not *culpable*, the police will probably say that…

Exercise V. Fill in the blank with the word from the Unit that best completes the sentence, using the root we supply as a clue. Then, answer the questions that follow the paragraphs.

The Promise of DNA Testing

Americans like to think that under our system of justice, ____*culprits*____ (CULP) are brought to trial, convicted, and punished. Yet the system is not perfect, and at times, in the presence of supposedly **incriminating** (CRIM) evidence, innocent people are swept up and wrongly convicted.

The science of DNA testing has been a major factor in changing the criminal justice system and determining responsibility for crimes. Supporters of such testing feel that it has provided scientific proof that our system routinely convicts and sentences innocent people, and that wrongful convictions are not the isolated or rare events they were once thought to be. Most important, DNA testing has opened a window into wrongful convictions so that the causes of such mistakes can be studied and remedies proposed.

Unfortunately, because of the ____*onerous*____ (ONER) expense of mounting a scientific defense, many people who could benefit from DNA testing have not had access to it. Part of the growing movement to reform the criminal justice system involves correcting such irregularities in the availability of technology. As an example, consider the Innocence Project at the Benjamin N. Cardoza School of Law.

The Innocence Project was set up as a nonprofit legal

clinic, and it handles only cases in which DNA testing may yield conclusive proof of guilt or innocence. At the clinic, students, overseen by a team of attorneys and clinic staff, handle the casework. Clients of the Project are generally people with very limited resources who have used up all of their other legal options. Many, it turns out, have been convicted on the grounds of mistaken identity or coerced confessions. Often, their last hope is that biological evidence from a case still exists for DNA testing.

Over the years, the Innocence Project has become more than a "court of last resort" for inmates who have exhausted their appeals and financial resources. The Project now helps law schools, journalism schools, and public defense offices across the country in proving the innocence of the wrongly convicted. To date, 128 people have been ***exonerated*** (ONER) through the work of the Innocence Project staff.

Because human beings, who inevitably make mistakes, govern U.S. courts, the probability of wrongful conviction in criminal cases will likely never be eliminated. However, as advancing science and technology take more and more of the guesswork out of investigations, unjust and erroneous verdicts will become more infrequent occurrences—so long as such technologies are within reach of all who need them.

1. Why does the author bring up the Innocence Project?
   A. as a way of explaining the beginnings of DNA testing
   B. ***to give an example of a trend in providing fair access to technology***
   C. to give an example of the movement to reform wrongly convicted defendants
   D. as a way of showing the Project's access to technology

2. Besides revealing the innocence of wrongly convicted persons, what other result does DNA testing have, according to the author?
   A. ***It allows a clearer understanding of why innocent people are found guilty.***
   B. It allows remedies for testing to be proposed.
   C. It shows that testing is not an isolated or rare event.
   D. It helps explain why innocent people want to be tested.

3. What is the purpose of the third paragraph?
   A. to explain why DNA testing is gaining supporters and note the supporters' arguments
   B. to warn that the courts will always make mistakes
   C. ***to explain why testing is not always available, and introduce one answer to the problem***
   D. to list reasons why someone would need DNA testing

4. Judging by this paragraph, what would earn the approbation of the Innocence Project staff?
   A. ***the government's establishment of a large fund for DNA testing***
   B. the advancement of DNA technology beyond the power of the court
   C. the allocation of financial resources to traditional investigating techniques
   D. the conviction of a person based on DNA testing

Exercise VI. Drawing on your knowledge of roots and words in context, read the following selection and define the *italicized* words. Note that the prefix *in* means "into, against." If you cannot figure out the meaning of the words on your own, look them up in a dictionary.

Answers will vary by student.

The primary goal of the District Attorney was to convince the jury to *inculpate* the defendant in the murder trial. In order to do this, the D.A. presented the results of the *probe* into the defendant's whereabouts on the day of the murder. Although this investigation did place the defendant away from the crime scene, the D.A. believed that he could disprove the defendant's alibi.

UNIT ELEVEN

FID
Latin **FIDERE, FISUS** "to trust, believe"

DIFFIDENT (dif´ i dənt) *adj.* Shy; not assertive
L. dis, "not," + fidere = *not trusting*
The young student, fearing the wrath of her teacher, spoke in a tiny, *diffident* voice.
syn: bashful   *ant:* confident

FIDELITY (fəd el´ ə tē) *n.* Faithfulness; loyalty
L. fidelis, "faithfulness," from fidere
The *fidelity* shown by the soldier was the subject of a book and a film.
                    ant: treachery

CONFIDE (kən fīd´) *v.* To trust (another) with information or a secret
L. con, "with," + fidus = *to be trusting with*
Gerri *confided* to me that she was very nervous about performing for the first time.
                    ant: conceal

FALL
Latin **FALLERE, FALSUM** "to deceive"

FALLACY (fal´ ə sē) *n.* A misleading or mistaken idea
L. fallax, "deceptive (idea)," from fallere
Even if I could convince myself that everyone feels the way I do, I would know in my heart that it was a *fallacy*.
syn: misconception   *ant:* truth

FALLACIOUS (fə lā´ shəs) *adj.* Misleading or deceptive
The council accused the businessman of unethical conduct and *fallacious* wording of contracts.

FALLIBLE (fal´ ə bəl) *adj.* Capable of being mistaken; imperfect
fallere + ible, "able to be" = *able to be deceived*
My brother strongly believed in the cause, but he was as *fallible* as any human being, and temptation led him astray.
                    ant: infallible, flawless

▣ *The official motto of the United States Marine Corps is "Semper Fidelis," which means "always faithful."*

▣ *We get the word "fail" from fallere.*

CRED
Latin **CREDERE, CREDITUM** "to trust, believe"

Although Sam told me that tires are EDIBLE, something tells me that isn't CREDIBLE.

CREDIBLE (kred´ i bəl) *adj.* Able to be trusted in or
      believed
L. credere + ible, "able to be" = *able to be believed*
Sam's story about the avalanche was amazing, but
credible.
syn: valid   *ant:* doubtful

CREDENCE (krē´ dəns) *n.* Trust or belief
I did not give *credence* to the rumors about the sheriff.
syn: acceptance   *ant:* mistrust

CREDULITY (krə jōō´ li tē) *n.* Tendency to believe things too quickly or easily
As Gabrielle grew older, she lost her innocent *credulity* and became more cynical
about people's intentions.
syn: gullibility   *ant:* skepticism

INCREDULOUS (in krej´ ə ləs) *adj.* Unable to believe something; amazed
L. in, "not," + credere = *not believing*
When Pete heard what I said, he gave me an *incredulous* stare.
syn: skeptical   *ant:* trusting

DUB
Latin **DUBIUS** "doubtful"
       DUBITARE, DUBITATUM, "to doubt"

DUBIOUS (dōō´ bē əs) *adj.* Uncertain; doubtful
Penny seemed rather *dubious* about the whole idea of skydiving.
syn: unconvinced   *ant:* positive

INDUBITABLE (in dōō´ bi tə bəl) *adj.* Certain beyond doubt or question
L. in, "not," + dubius = *not able to be doubted*
The mechanic was a man of *indubitable* loyalty.
syn: absolute   *ant:* unsure

REDOUBTABLE (rē dout´ ə bəl) *adj.* Worthy of fear or respect; mighty
Middle French redouter, "dread," (from Latin re, "again," + dubius, "doubt")
Even the most *redoubtable* of the warriors did not last very long in the blizzard.
syn: formidable

▥ *"Doubt" also comes from*
dubitare. *If you have
trouble remembering the
meaning of* redoubtable,
*just think of something
so powerful that it makes
you doubt yourself again
and again.*

EXERCISES - UNIT ELEVEN

Exercise I. Complete the sentence in a way that shows you understand the meaning of the italicized vocabulary word. *Answers will vary by student.*

1. Because of the *credence* the townspeople gave to the stories of witchcraft, they...

2. When I said that her argument constituted a logical *fallacy*, Mariah responded that...

3. One thing that made George painfully aware of how *fallible* he really could be was...

4. Although Risa has developed a *credible* theory about weather patterns,...

5. Because of the *credulity* Fiona displayed when her peers told her made-up stories, they...

6. The *fallacious* reasoning in the essay on American politics might lead the reader to...

7. When the doctor noticed his patient looking *dubious* about the surgery, he...

8. Leon's *fidelity* and trustworthiness when it came to minding the company's finances made him...

9. Only the most *redoubtable* athletes are able to...

10. Because Louisa's fellow students considered her rather *diffident*, they often...

11. If I *confide* in you regarding the major new plan to restructure the city, I expect you to...

12. It is *indubitable* that the world will see another war sometime in the future, because...

13. Veronica was *incredulous* at the sight of the volcano because...

Exercise II. Fill in the blank with the best word from the choices below. One word will not be used.

    fidelity   redoubtable   dubious   confide   diffident

1. Although she looked __*dubious*__ when I suggested climbing the fence, Lizzie went along with the plan.

2. The __*fidelity*__ you displayed when your friends were in danger shows me how loyal you really are.

3. I hope that Andrew will not __*confide*__ in Jeff, since Jeff has a reputation for spreading other people's secrets around.

4. The army was facing its most __*redoubtable*__ foe, a force almost three times bigger than itself.

Fill in the blank with the best word from the choices below. One word will not be used.

      fallacy   diffident   fallacious   credulity   indubitable

5.   That the evidence was falsified now seems ___*indubitable*___.

6.   Dr. Leary's more ___*diffident*___ patients are sometimes too shy or nervous to ask questions about their health.

7.   The ___*credulity*___ which you showed to the car salesman will make him think he can overcharge you.

8.   Do not try to undermine my point with ___*fallacious*___ logic and unreliable evidence.

Fill in the blank with the best word from the choices below. One word will not be used.

      fallible   credible   credence   dubious   fallacy

9.   The detective thought the witness' story was ___*credible*___ enough.

10.   Until I fell in love with someone who was totally uninterested in me, I really didn't think I was ___*fallible*___.

11.   How much ___*credence*___ do you give to the flashy stories you see on the local news?

12.   Although the salesman's pitch was convincing, it was based on a ___*fallacy*___.

Exercise III. Choose the set of words that best completes the sentence.

1.   Although he was quiet, even _____, in school, Vince became a(n) _____ warrior on the football field.
    A. fallacious; incredulous
    B. indubitable; dubious
    C. diffident; redoubtable
    D. fallible; indubitable

2.   Although some of the group found the story _____, other members were highly _____ about it.
    A. diffident; credible
    B. redoubtable; fallacious
    C. incredulous; fallible
    D. credible; dubious

3. Henry knew himself to be _____, but he was _____ when he heard about the mistake he had made.
   A. redoubtable; fallible
   B. fallacious; diffident
   C. credible; diffident
   D. fallible; incredulous

4. When Mary _____ in me that she could fly, I wondered if she were testing my _____.
   A. confided; diffidence
   B. confided; fallacy
   C. confided; credulity
   D. confided; fidelity

5. After the secret agent was accused of spying on his own country, everyone thought he was of _____ _____, and no one trusted him.
   A. fallacious; credulity
   B. dubious; fidelity
   C. credible; fallacy
   D. redoubtable; credulity

Exercise IV. Complete the sentence by drawing an inference about the *italicized* word from its context.

Answers will vary by student.

1. If Norman looks *incredulous* when he hears about his salary raise, we can infer that his raise is...

2. When a reviewer says that a play's magnificence is *indubitable*, he probably believes that...

3. If a farmer refuses to give *credence* to a report about livestock illness, he might be assuming that...

Exercise V. Fill in the blank with the word from the Unit that best completes the sentence, using the root we supply as a clue. Then, answer the questions that follow the paragraphs.

The Lasting Influence of Richard Nixon

Since President Richard Nixon resigned in shame from office in 1973, the American public has generally held the opinion that elected officials are ___*fallible*___.(FALL) This was a common enough opinion before Nixon, but it was the Watergate scandal that really affected of all of Nixon's successors and made voters understand that presidents were, first and foremost, politicians. After Watergate, the President's solemn oath to "preserve, protect, and defend the Constitution of the United States" sounded like little more than empty repetition of a vow. The Commander-in-Chief seemed to be primarily in the service of his own interests and agenda, rather than the service of the citizens whom he represented.

Presidents are expected to exhibit a high level of ___*fidelity*___ (FID) to the American people as well as to the Constitution. Accordingly, they must monitor all of their own actions, both public and private, with the utmost scrutiny. In Nixon's case, several high-level officials of his administration were indirectly involved in an attempt to obtain information illegally from Nixon's Democratic opponents. The material the burglars collected was to be used in Nixon's upcoming reelection campaign. The scheme was exposed when a night watchman became aware of a burglary at the Watergate Hotel, where the Democratic National Committee had its headquarters. To compound matters, Nixon, attempting to conceal his own administration's involvement in the burglary, instigated a massive cover-up of the facts.

Nixon was formally impeached, but before the Senate could remove him from office, he resigned. The idea that the highest-ranking elected representative of the American people could be involved in something as obviously criminal as breaking-and-entering was severely damaging to the trust Americans had for all elected officials. Succeeding presidents attempted to win back the favor and faith of their populace, but generally wound up losing their good reputations in one scandal after another. Ronald Reagan, for instance, was deeply involved in the Iran-Contra scandal; Bill Clinton was continually investigated for financial misdeeds and personal misconduct.

Many Americans surveyed in the years since Richard Nixon's resignation have admitted that they do not find many of the White House's promises _credible_ (CRED); in fact, surveys show that most citizens are _dubious_ (DUB) about the honesty of elected officials in general. Such is the unfortunate legacy of the Watergate scandal.

1. Which sentence below best sums up a main idea of the passage?
   A. The American people are skeptical by nature.
   B. *The American people are cynical as a result of experience.*
   C. The American people are troubled by the idea of elected officials.
   D. The American people repeatedly betray their politicians.

2. The voters found out that Richard Nixon was fallible when he
   A. was elected to the Presidency.
   B. took the vow to uphold the Constitution.
   C. decided to resign from office.
   D. *was shown to be connected to the Watergate burglary.*

3. Which of the following was a side effect of the Watergate scandal?
   A. Democrats ceased trusting in any Republican official.
   B. American voters began to have negative feelings about earlier Presidents.
   C. *Succeeding elected officials did not have the trust of the American people.*
   D. A night watchman discovered a burglary at the Watergate hotel.

Exercise VI. Drawing on your knowledge of roots and words in context, read the following selection and define the *italicized* words. Note that the prefix *ac* (from *ad*) means "toward" and the prefix *in* means "not."

   Answers will vary by student.

During the Protestant Reformation, many Christians deserted the Catholic Church. Growing distrust of the Church led these men and women to branch off and start their own sects. The Pope did not *accredit* these sects. Because the Protestants did not have the approval of the Pope, many Catholics considered them *infidels*.

UNIT TWELVE

ULTIMA
Latin **ULTIMUS** "last"

III *The* ultima *of a word is its final syllable; the pen-ultima is the next-to-last syllable.*

ULTIMATE (ul´ tə mət) *adj.* Surpassing all others; definitive
L. ultimus = *having a final quality*
The *ultimate* humiliation came when Robbie's teacher yelled at him in front of the whole class.

PENULTIMATE (pen ul´ tə mət) *adj.* Just before the final; next to last
L. paene, "almost," + ultimus = *the next to last*
In the *penultimate* chapter of the book, the author prepares us for the shocking twists of the final chapter.

ULTIMATUM (ul tə māt´ əm) *n.* A demand or threat that is final
L. ultimus (*that which is*) *final*
The pirates gave us an *ultimatum*: either reveal where the prisoners were, or walk the plank.

FIN
Latin **FINIS** "end, border, limit"

INFINITE (in´ fə nit) *adj.* Without beginning or end
L. in, "not," + finis = (*having*) *no end*
Although Seth was a man of seemingly *infinite* patience, he sometimes became frustrated.

DEFINITIVE (dē fin´ ə tiv) *adj.* Defining for all others; standard
L. de, "from," + finis = (*measurable*) *from its limits*
John did not consider the work a *definitive* authority on the history of tennis.
syn: absolute   *ant:* uncertain

INFINITESIMAL (in fin i tes´ ə məl) *adj.* Extremely small; incalculably or immeasurably small
L. in, "not," + finis = (*so small as to have*) *no measure*
If any of the contaminant is left in the water supply, it is there only in *infinitesimal* amounts.
syn: microscopic   *ant:* huge

NOV
Latin **NOVUS** "new"

NOVEL (näv´ əl) *adj.* New and different
The company had a *novel* approach to the problem of engine breakdown.
syn: original   *ant*: stale

NOVICE (näv´ is) *n.* An inexperienced person; amateur
L. novitia, "one who is new," from novus
Even I, a chess *novice*, could appreciate the beauty of the master's play.
syn: beginner   *ant*: expert

The NOVICE gangster had
"NO VICE" yet.

INNOVATIVE (in ə vā´ tiv) *adj.* Showing creativity and originality
L. in, "intensive," + novus = *very new*
The *innovative* design of the new C-267 makes it the easiest vacuum cleaner to use.
syn: inventive   *ant*: conservative

PRIM
Latin **PRIMUS** "first"

PRIMAL (prī´ məl) *adj.* Original; dating from the beginning of existence
Fear is one of our more *primal* emotions; it helped our ancient ancestors survive.
syn: primitive   *ant*: modern

PRIMEVAL (prī mē´vəl) *adj.* Extremely ancient; of earliest time
L. primus + aevum, "age" = *[dating from] the first age*
The rough cliffs had a *primeval* splendor that made us think of the beginning of time.
syn: primordial

PRIMACY (prī´ mə sē) *n.* Condition of being first in time or importance
No one dared question the *primacy* of the police captain in the precinct.

EXERCISES - UNIT TWELVE

Exercise I. Complete the sentence in a way that shows you understand the meaning of the italicized vocabulary word. *Answers will vary by student.*

1. Corey considered losing the class presidency the *ultimate* regret of his life, since he...

2. Emotions like fear and hatred are often referred to as *primal* because...

3. The advertisement claimed that the design of the computer was *novel* because...

4. Maria started to believe that her father's financial resources were *infinite* because...

5. The *primeval* beauty of the ancient forest reminded Sharon that...

6. When our manager heard some of the *innovative* ideas we had come up with, he...

7. If the workers who are on strike do not follow their employer's *ultimatum*...

8. As a *novice* on the ski slopes, I often...

9. Because the students were only in the *penultimate* rehearsal for the play, they...

10. Mr. Wendal became the *definitive* expert on whales and dolphins by...

11. Members of the rebel army started to question the *primacy* of their leader because...

12. Because the amount of water on the foreign planet was *infinitesimal*, the explorers...

Exercise II. Fill in the blank with the best word from the choices below. One word will not be used.

infinitesimal   infinite   penultimate   primal   novel

1. The microscope was so powerful that it allowed us to see things of an almost __*infinitesimal*__ size.

2. The __*penultimate*__ surprise came when we found our dog was going to have puppies, but the final shock was that our cat was going to have kittens at the same time.

3. I felt a surge of raw, __*primal*__ anger when I saw that my house had been destroyed.

4. Early astronomers argued over whether the universe was __*infinite*__ or had limits.

Fill in the blank with the best word from the choices below. One word will not be used.

     novice   infantile   ultimatum   primacy   novel

5.   Percy still needs help with his free throws because he is a basketball ___*novice*___.

6.   The general issued a(n) ___*ultimatum*___ to the enemy soldiers: they could lay down their weapons or be fired upon.

7.   The minister warned that the ___*primacy*___ of spiritual laws cannot be forgotten, even when day-to-day life becomes difficult.

8.   One ___*novel*___ solution to the arguments that broke out at every meeting was to give each club member a speaking time in advance.

Fill in the blank with the best word from the choices below. One word will not be used.

     innovative   definitive   penultimate   ultimate   primeval

9.   Because Julio is so shy, public speaking seems like the ___*ultimate*___ torture to him.

10. The ___*definitive*___ book on how to make pizza was written by a man who owned a pizza parlor for many years.

11. One of the most ___*innovative*___ uses of technology that I saw at the computer showcase was a program that helps blind children learn to read.

12. The statue in the museum was a representation of a(n) ___*primeval*___ god of fire.

Exercise III. Choose the set of words that best completes the sentence.

1.   The _____ of freedom in the minds of the people was clear when they issued a(n) _____ to the tyrant.
     A. novice; ultimatum
     B. ultimatum; novice
     C. *primacy; ultimatum*
     D. affinity; novice

2.   One of the most _____ features of the new machine was that, unlike the old model, it released only_____ amounts of harmful chemicals.
     A. *novel; infinitesimal*
     B. definitive; penultimate
     C. primeval; novel
     D. primeval; definitive

3. The psychologist has written the _____ work on _____ emotions like fear, hate, and desire.
   A. primeval; novel
   B. penultimate; ultimate
   C. novel; infinitesimal
   D. definitive; primal

4. As a(n) _____ in swimming, I was given the _____ thrill when I got to meet the Olympic swimming champion.
   A. ultimatum; definitive
   B. novice; ultimate
   C. ultimatum; primeval
   D. novice; primeval

5. I was amazed at some of the _____ uses the ancient people had found for the _____ sur-roundings.
   A. primeval; definitive
   B. innovative; primeval
   C. ultimate; definitive
   D. novel; penultimate

Exercise IV. Complete the sentence by drawing an inference about the *italicized* word from its context.

   Answers will vary by student.

1. If Regan hears someone on the television describing *primeval* hunters, she will probably think of...

2. Charles is upset because he lost to a *novice* chess player, and he probably believes that...

3. If a noted history scholar calls a particular research paper *definitive*, he is probably recommending that...

Exercise V. Fill in the blank with the word from the Unit that best completes the sentence, using the root we supply as a clue. Then, answer the questions that follow the paragraphs.

A Devout and Compassionate Life

Albert Schweitzer, noted scholar, musician, doctor, and humanitarian, felt that his life was directed by divine call-ing. Even his many secular interests seem to have been colored by religious yearning. His numerous scholarly and humanitarian achievements were spread among several fields, but all originated in one central, spiritual motivation.

Schweitzer first chose to conduct his investigation of morality and divinity through scholarship. At the age of eighteen, he enrolled at the University of Strasbourg in Germany; six years later, he had earned a doctorate in phi-losophy. Additional study at the Sorbonne in France and the University of Berlin gained him an advanced degree in the-ology. At 27, he decided to accept the appointment of prin-cipal at St. Thomas College in Strasbourg, where his duties included lecturing in philosophy and theology. Before he was thirty years old, Schweitzer would publish several **_definitive_** (FIN) books on theology, including *The Quest for the Historical Jesus* and *The Mysticism of Paul the Apostle*.

At the same time that he was pursuing his degrees, Schweitzer was becoming an authority on the construction and music of the organ. His deep love for the instrument led him to a mastery of organ music, and then to the publica-tion of a book concerning the works of the composer Johann Sebastian Bach. In these endeavors, as in his studies, he did not neglect the spiritual aspect of his subject. His book pri-marily considers the religious nature of Bach's compositions.

His next career was neither in music or theology, but still originated in Schweitzer's meditations on faith. After coming across a missionary publication containing an appeal for doctors in French Equatorial Africa, he decided to devote his life to practicing medicine in that region. Schweitzer's careful consideration of civilization and ethics convinced him that white, Christian society was stifling the dignity of non-white cultures and ethnicities and preventing such cultures from advancing. He wrote two books in which he explored the theory that the decay of civilization was a result of the lack of "reverence for life." Having put forth some of his own ideas about the gross injustice he had discovered, he made known his plan to become a surgeon, and to practice in the jungles of Africa.

When he was 38 years old, Albert Schweitzer carried out his plan. Armed with knowledge of and experience in medicine and surgery, he built a hospital in the French Congo. There he and his wife Helene, often operating under difficult conditions and in unsanitary environments, treated lepers and other patients. This work was to occupy Schweitzer for the rest of his life.

Albert Schweitzer's philosophy of compassion and respect for all humans, in addition to his many written works, won him the Nobel Peace Prize in 1952. It is clear, though, that recognition, whether for achievements in theological study, music, or medicine, meant far less to Schweitzer than the opportunity to exercise and understand religious devotion and compassion. His **novel/innovative** (NOV) ideas about the purpose of human life changed the way scholars and humanitarians thought about their mission in life. Many people are still following his example today.

1. According to the passage, which of the following statements about Schweitzer is true?
   A. He was a professor of music and a Lutheran minister.
   B. *He was a man of many talents as well as a humanitarian.*
   C. He became a doctor after a missionary society rejected him.
   D. His musical talent kept him from being a doctor at an early age.

2. What is the main idea of the passage?
   A. Albert Schweitzer was interested in the theology of Johann Sebastian Bach.
   B. Albert Schweitzer was both scholar and humanitarian.
   C. Albert Schweitzer chose religion over medicine.
   D. *Albert Schweitzer lived according to his religious beliefs.*

3. What is one way that the author proves the statement, "Even his many secular interests seemed to have been colored by religious yearning"?
   A. *by describing Schweitzer's study of the religious aspects of Bach*
   B. by noting the conditions under which Schweitzer operated
   C. by revealing that Schweitzer was the son of a Lutheran pastor
   D. by noting Schweitzer's disregard for awards

Exercise VI. Drawing on your knowledge of roots and words in context, read the following selection and define the *italicized* words. Note that the suffix – *ordial* comes from the Latin *ordior* meaning, "to begin." In addition, the prefix *re* means "again, back." If you cannot figure out the meaning of the words on your own, look them up in a dictionary.

Answers will vary by student.

The rainforests of South America and Southeast Asia are considered by many scientists the closest we will ever get to true *primordial* landscapes in the modern world. Unfortunately, as man continues to search for new sources of medicines, animal species, and wood, these rainforests are quickly being destroyed. Many fear that in a few years, trees from the rainforest, having all been harvested for use in home *renovations*, will no longer shelter exotic birds. Environmentalists warn that we should no longer seek to update our created world at the expense of the natural one.

UNIT THIRTEEN

ERR
Latin ERRARE, ERRATUM "to wander"

ABERRANT (a ber´ ənt) *adj.* Deviating from a pattern or rule
L. ab, "away from," + errare = *wandering away from*
Since the data had previously been so consistent, the *aberrant* results puzzled the scientists.
syn: abnormal   *ant:* typical

ERRONEOUS (e rō´ nē əs) *adj.* Wrong or inaccurate
L. erronis (from errare) = *straying from (the correct rule or standard)*
Tina came to the understandable but *erroneous* conclusion that all dogs were unfriendly.
syn: mistaken   *ant:* correct

ERRANT (er´ ənt) *adj.* Wandering or straying
The *errant* knight soon found more adventure than he had bargained for.
syn: wayward   *ant:* on course

GRAD/GRESS
Latin GRADI, GRESSUM "to go forth, to proceed"

DEGRADE (dē grād´) *v.* To lower in dignity or esteem; insult
L. de, "down," + gradi = *(to cause to) go down*
Hannah felt that the mayor's comment *degraded* women and should be withdrawn.
syn: belittle   *ant:* honor

CONGRESS (kon´ gris) *n.* A coming together
L. con, "together," + gressum = *a proceeding together*
The meeting of scientists was hailed as "a *congress* of great minds."

EGRESS (ē´ gres) *n.* Act of going out; exit
L. e, "out of," + gressum = *going out*
The prisoners were given *egress* after their court hearing.

▥ *A famous line from the poet Alexander Pope's* Essay on Criticism *states that "to err is human, to forgive divine."*

▥ *P.T. Barnum, the famous showman, had a problem: customers were flocking to his sideshows in such numbers that they clogged his building, and newer customers could not come in. So he put up a sign reading "This way to egress." His patrons, not knowing the meaning of "egress," eagerly followed the sign, expecting an exotic animal. They soon found themselves out on the street.*

VEN/VENT

Latin **VENIRE, VENTUM** "to come"

CONVENE (kən vēn´) *v.* To call together, to assemble
L. con, "together," + venire = *to come together*
With the ringing of the bell, our chairman *convened* the fifth annual workshop.
syn: gather   *ant:* adjourn

COVENANT (kəv´ ən ənt) *n.* A mutual or legal agreement
Because the ancient *covenant* between the two tribes had been broken, a special meeting had to be called.
syn: contract   *ant:* break off

CIRCUMVENT (sûr kəm vent´) *v.* To avoid by going around; bypass
L. circum, "around," + ventum = *to go around*
Harold attempted to *circumvent* the problem by planning ahead.
syn: sidestep   *ant:* confront

The traffic had to CIRCUMVENT the CIRCUS TENT that was set up in the middle of Main Street.

CUR/CURS

Latin **CURRERE, CURSUM** "to run"

CURSORY (kûr´ sə rē) *adj.* Hasty and superficial
Diane gave me a *cursory* wave as she was whisked away into the ballroom.
syn: casual   *ant:* comprehensive

PRECURSOR (prē kûr´ sər) *n.* That which comes before; forerunner
L. pre, "before," + currere = *running before*
The shower of hail was only a *precursor* to the worst storm we had ever seen.
syn: harbinger

RECOURSE (rē´ kôrs) *n.* Help for a problem; solution
L. re, "back," + currere = *running back*
When Cameron needed help building the house, his only *recourse* was to go to his brother.
syn: resource

INCURSION (in kûr´ zhən) *n.* An attack on another's territory; a raid
Latin in, "into," + currere = *running into*
The soldier surveyed the damage after the enemy *incursion*.
syn: invasion

▥ *How do you think a noun literally meaning "a running back" came to mean "solution to a problem"?*

EXERCISES - UNIT THIRTEEN

Exercise I. Complete the sentence in a way that shows you understand the meaning of the italicized vocabulary word. *Answers will vary by student.*

1.   The policeman feared that the minor crimes were *precursors* to larger ones because...

2.   Mary felt that the magazine article *degraded* scientists because it said...

3.   Although he did all he could to *circumvent* the city traffic, Mike...

4.   My last *recourse* when I couldn't get my car started was to...

5.   When Rose told Catherine about the tooth fairy, Catherine made the *erroneous* assumption that...

6.   We later learned that the *errant* golf ball that had struck a passerby was...

7.   Because I did only a *cursory* reading of the instructions on the test, I...

8.   A *congress* of local citizens gathered in the town square was able to...

9.   The right of *egress* was denied to the man accused of the crime because...

10. When the king wanted to *convene* a council of wise men, he...

11. Since none of the survey results on television we have gathered seems to be *aberrant*, we know that...

12. If there is to be a *covenant* between the two nations, they must...

Exercise II. Fill in the blank with the best word from the choices below. One word will not be used.

aberrant   errant   egress   circumvent   cursory

1.   If the **_errant_** bullet had not hit a wall, someone could have been seriously injured.

2.   If we meet their demands, the hostage-takers will give the hostages **_egress_**.

3.   Even a(n) **_cursory_** glance at the room told the detective that something had gone horribly wrong.

4.   Is there any way to **_circumvent_** the floods that come in the spring?

Fill in the blank with the best word from the choices below. One word will not be used.

> covenant   congress   precursor   degrade   incursion

5. A small _____*congress*_____ of local merchants had appeared on the village green.

6. When the sacred _____*covenant*_____ between a ruler and his or her people is broken, the consequences can be severe.

7. The reviewer went so far as to personally _____*degrade*_____ many actors, calling them "unfit to take the stage."

8. A(n) _____*incursion*_____ into the camp of the enemy helped the soldiers gain valuable information and supplies.

Fill in the blank with the best word from the choices below. One word will not be used.

> cursory   erroneous   convened   recourse   precursor   aberrant

9. When the medical tests showed that Ron was severely ill, he felt sure the results were _____*erroneous*_____.

10. Compared to the rest of the cells we have collected, this cell, which is much bigger, seems _____*aberrant*_____.

11. The judge _____*convened*_____ the court session by pounding her gavel.

12. The horse and buggy was a(n) _____*precursor*_____ to our modern automobile.

13. Harriet felt she had no _____*recourse*_____ but to go to the police with her information.

Exercise III. Choose the set of words that best completes the sentence.

1. I don't mean to _____ our lecturer, but I think some of his conclusions were _____.
    A. convene; aberrant
    B. circumvent; errant
    C. convene; errant
    D. degrade; erroneous

2. The first meeting that they _____ was only a(n) _____ to a much larger one later held that day.
    A. degraded; precursor
    B. convened; precursor
    C. degraded; covenant
    D. circumvented; egress

3.   When the sacred _____ between Lucile and her true love was broken, she felt she had no _____ except to find comfort in the church.
     A. **covenant; recourse**
     B. congress; covenant
     C. precursor; incursion
     D. recourse; precursor

4.   The journalists visiting the war-torn country were denied _____ and decided to _____ the ruling by sneaking out of the country at night.
     A. precursor; convene
     B. covenant; degrade
     C. **egress; circumvent**
     D. incursion; degrade

5.   The soldier captured behind enemy lines denied he was on a(n) _____ into enemy territory; he said he was merely a(n) _____ traveler.
     A. covenant; aberrant
     B. **incursion; errant**
     C. precursor; cursory
     D. congress; cursory

Exercise IV. Complete the sentence by drawing an inference about the *italicized* word from its context.

   Answers will vary by student.

1.   When Rob walks into a room where a camera has been secretly hidden and gives a *cursory* glance around the room, we can assume that...

2.   Immigrants who watch a television show that *degrades* people who legally come to America will likely...

3.   If a geologist testing the soil comes up with test results that seem to be *aberrant*, the geologist will probably...

Exercise V. Fill in the blank with the word from the Unit that best completes the sentence, using the root we supply as a clue. Then, answer the questions that follow the paragraphs.

The Uncertain Success of Title IX

In 1972, Congress, in an effort to end gender inequality in our nation's schools, approved the bill now known as Title IX. Leading to the passage of this law was the realization that young women did not have the academic, career, and sports opportunities afforded to their male peers. Title IX was controversial from the beginning, but nowhere did its implications meet with more resistance than in organized sports programs within the public schools.

High school sports have long been the domain of the male student population. It is boys' sports such as football that not only attract major crowds, but also serve as profitable enterprises for many large high school sports programs.

Title IX has brought more money to women's sports, but it has not solved the gender gap.

Girls are still unable to find acceptance on traditionally male sports teams. In 1972, it was impossible for a female student to earn a spot on a high school football team. In 2003, there are only a handful of young women who have earned the right to play football. Although girls' basketball is common, only rarely does a girl play basketball on the boys' team. Boys' basketball is more prestigious than girls', and remains more likely to attract attention and money to the school and individual players.

Young female athletes face sparse crowds and little support from school and parental organizations. While attendance at a boys' sports event may be standing room only, there are rarely sold-out crowds for even the best teams in girls' sports. The absence of fans to support winning teams in girls' sports is ___degrading___ (GRAD) to these young people.

In addition, because girls' sports have not yet gained the attention that traditional boys' sports have, there is less scholarship money available for women athletes. 72% of high school athletic scholarships are still awarded to boys. Young women with athletic talents occasionally do win these awards, but usually end up earning less money and prestige.

Although Title IX has made sports and other opportunities more accessible to young women, thirty years after its passage its benefits are still relatively insignificant. Many believe, ___erroneously___ (ERR), that Title IX brought gender equity to sports programs and individuals in our public schools. Until society accepts the value of girls in sports, young women will not have earned the equality promised by Title IX.

1. According to the author, Title IX's success rate has been
    A. outstanding.
    B. _fair._
    C. poor.
    D. average.

2. Which sentence best describes the main idea of this piece?
    A. In 1972, Congress passed Title IX in an effort to end gender inequality in our nation's schools.
    B. High school sports have long been the domain of the male student population.
    C. _Thirty years after Title IX's passage, its benefits are still relatively insignificant._
    D. Girls are still unable to find acceptance on traditionally boys' sports teams.

3. Gender equality in girls' sports is measured by
    A. attendance at sporting events.
    B. scholarships and recognition.
    C. attitudes of fellow students, parents, and society.
    D. _All of the above_

4. Which of the following statements is NOT true, according to the passage?
    A. Title IX is controversial thirty years after its passage.
    B. _Boys' sports are more important than girls' sports._
    C. 38% of athletic scholarships are awarded to girls.
    D. Girls can and do play on some boys' sports teams.

Exercise VI. Drawing on your knowledge of roots and words in context, read the following selection and define the _italicized_ words. Note that the prefix _re_ means "back," and _trans_ means "beyond." If you cannot figure out the meaning of the words on your own, look them up in a dictionary.

Answers will vary by student.

During the latest three-day outdoor music festival known as Woodstock, many people at the concert _regressed_ to primitive behavior. The crowd of young adults and teenagers acted more like untamed beasts than civilized human beings. Their uncontrolled behavior, ranging from rioting to rolling in the mud, _transgressed_ the rules of social acceptability. Following the festival, there was a movement toward more crowd control and tighter security at concerts.

UNIT FOURTEEN

VIR
Latin **VIR** "man"

VIRILE (vēr´ əl) *adj.* Masculine; manly
Will tried to prove he was strong and *virile* by lifting the enormous refrigerator.

When Eric looked in the mirror, he saw a VIRILE VIKING.

VIRTUE (vûr´ chōō) *n.* Right action; moral goodness
It takes a special kind of *virtue* to do good acts and never seek recognition for them.

VIRTUOSO (vûr chōō ō´ sō) *n.* Someone extraordinarily skilled in a particular art
Frank was a piano *virtuoso*; he could play extraordinarily difficult pieces by ear.

DEM
Greek **DEMOS** "people"

DEMAGOGUE (dem´ ə gäg) *n.* A leader who appeals to people's emotions to gain power
G. demos + agein, "to lead" = *one who leads people*
Some voters feared our governor, whose opinions seemed to change depending on his audience, was in danger of becoming a *demagogue*.

DEMOGRAPHIC (dem ə graf´ ik) *adj.* Having certain characteristics in common, such as age, race, or gender
G. demos + graphy, "study of" = *study of people*
The company targeted a very specific *demographic* group with a new series of advertisements aimed at teenagers.

PANDEMIC (pan dem´ ik) *adj.* Having an effect on a large area or region
G. pan, "all," + demos = *all people*
The mysterious disease seemed to be *pandemic* among the inhabitants of the country.
syn: rampant   *ant:* confined

To the Romans, a vir was a man, and virtus, *which came into English as virtue, was all that was best about a man's physical and moral being: courage, strength, skill, nobility. Today, of course, both men and women can be virtuous.*

Democracy, literally meaning "power of the people," is what allows us all to have a say in our government. But a demagogue, a "people leader," takes advantage of the people to gain power for himself or herself.

In order to successfully sell a product, a marketing professional must think of the demographic group that will receive the advertisement. If a commercial on television, for instance, is shown to senior citizens, but is designed for a demographic group that includes children, the product will probably not sell very well.

POLIT
Greek **POLIS** "city"

COSMOPOLITAN (käz mə päl´ it ən) *adj.* Worldly or sophisticated
G. cosmos, "world," + polis = *being a citizen of the world*
While Wendy's husband thought the restaurant had an appealing *cosmopolitan* flavor, Wendy's mother thought the whole place rather snobbish.
syn: cultured   *ant:* unpolished

POLITICIZE (pəl it´ i sīz) *v.* To give a political character to something.
Some people criticize the President for *politicizing* an otherwise neutral situation

APOLITICAL (ā pəl it´ i kəl) *adj.* Having no interest in politics; not political
G. a, "not," + politikos (from polis) = *not political*
Many people who were once *apolitical* turned out to vote in the recent elections.

CIVIS
Latin **CIVIS** "citizen"

CIVILITY (si vil´ i tē) *n.* Politeness; courteousness
Although my brother and I fought constantly, we treated each other with *civility* in public.
syn: decorum   *ant:* rudeness

CIVIC (siv´ ik) *adj.* Having to do with the business of a town or community
Mrs. Morita considers it her *civic* duty to attend the town meetings.

CIVILIZE (siv´ ə līz) *v.* To make more cultured or refined
My mother's attempt to *civilize* her wild children only made us more determined to do whatever we wanted.
syn: polish

▥ *In ancient Greece, the polis, or city-state, was the center of government, art and culture (Athens and Sparta are the two most famous examples). Just as a voting member of one of our modern cities is a citizen, a voting member of the polis was called a politikos. We get our word* political *from* politikos.

EXERCISES - UNIT FOURTEEN

Exercise I. Complete the sentence in a way that shows you understand the meaning of the italicized vocabulary word. *Answers will vary by student.*

1.   To express their *civic* pride, the Johnson family...

2.   With her stylish car and *cosmopolitan* wardrobe, Bette looked like someone who...

3.   Many fans considered Jimmy a tennis *virtuoso* because he...

4.   The *demographic* group targeted by the ice-cream company was...

5.   A small group of citizens tried to *politicize* the town meeting by...

6.   We could tell the young wrestler was *virile* because he...

7.   The most important *virtue* to have as a firefighter is probably...

8.   The pioneers tried to *civilize* the frontier by...

9.   Although the charity organization claimed to be *apolitical*...

10.   Because Margaret exercised *civility* towards Troy after he had hurt her feelings, Troy...

11.   A rabble-rouser and a *demagogue*, the candidate traveled around the state, looking to...

12.   Once the doctors were certain that polio was *pandemic* in the city's population, they...

Exercise II. Fill in the blank with the best word from the choices below. One word will not be used.

politicize   virtue   virtuoso   pandemic   civilize

1.   It would be unfortunate if money were able to __*politicize*__ a group that has worked so hard to avoid endorsing a candidate.

2.   If I cannot __*civilize*__ my rowdy dogs within a few weeks, my neighbors are going to start complaining.

3.   Patience was a __*virtue*__ that my grandmother had in abundance.

4.   The speaker said that greed, like a disease, is__*pandemic*__ in the Western world.

Fill in the blank with the best word from the choices below. One word will not be used.

civic   virile   demographic   demagogue   apolitical

5. Do you think the President is charming and charismatic, or is he a(n) ___demagogue___ who might eventually abuse the power he gains?

6. To what ___demographic___ group is this political campaign appealing?

7. To prove that he is ___virile___, a male gorilla will beat his chest and tear leaves from the trees.

8. Oliver, who once considered himself ___apolitical___, is now campaigning for governor.

Fill in the blank with the best word from the choices below. One word will not be used.

virtuoso   civilize   civic   cosmopolitan   civility

9. To Libbie, taking a limousine uptown felt very glamorous and ___cosmopolitan___.

10. Roger felt it was his ___civic___ responsibility to pick up litter and sweep the sidewalk in the town.

11. Rather than trying to prove she was a ballet ___virtuoso___, Amelia decided to show the audition judges the passion she felt for her art.

12. If Liam and Jane could show ___civility___ to one another for even a minute, there would be no more fighting in the house.

Exercise III. Choose the set of words that best completes the sentence.

1. One _____ of being as _____ as my uncle is having the ability to share interesting information about the world.
   A. demagogue; apolitical
   B. virtue; cosmopolitan
   C. virtuoso; civic
   D. demographic; civil

2. When Annette refused to criticize any of the local candidates, was she being _____ or just _____ and polite?
   A. cosmopolitan; civic
   B. demographic; virile
   C. virile; pandemic
   D. apolitical; civil

3. Although the general said he was using force and strict laws to _____ the country, some people feared he was a _____ who would abuse his power.
    A. civilize; virtuoso
    B. pandemic; virtue
    C. civilize; demagogue
    D. demographic; pandemic

4. We knew that repression had become _____ when even a shy little flute _____ was arrested for anti-government activities.
    A. pandemic; virtuoso
    B. demographic; cosmopolitan
    C. virile; demagogue
    D. politic; virtuoso

5. A group of _____-minded local citizens published a report on the various _____ groups in the town.
    A. virile; apolitical
    B. cosmopolitan; civic
    C. civic; demographic
    D. demagogue; pandemic

Exercise IV. Complete the sentence by drawing an inference about the *italicized* word from its context.

   Answers will vary by student.

1. If someone driving by a billboard sees that it features a tractor, a cornfield, and a barn, he or she might assume the *demographic* group being targeted by the billboard is...

2. Listening to a recording of a guitarist, Joe exclaimed, "What a *virtuoso*!" We can assume the guitarist is...

3. When a teacher in a kindergarten class wants her students to use *civility* towards one another, she will probably encourage them to...

Exercise V. Fill in the blank with the word from the Unit that best completes the sentence, using the root we supply as a clue. Then, answer the questions that follow the paragraphs.

Religion and Government in America

Among the first European settlers in America were the Puritans, who, fleeing religious persecution in Europe, settled the Massachusetts Bay Colony in 1630. John Winthrop, their leader, was a religious man who later became the Governor of the Massachusetts Bay Colony. As the colonists were making their way across the Atlantic Ocean, Winthrop delivered a sermon to them containing his vision of what the new country was to be like. It would be a place, he said, where people would be allowed to worship as they chose, but the government would be partially controlled by the church. John Winthrop and the Puritans did not imagine any separation between religious and ___**civic**___ (CIV) institutions in the new America. The country had to go through many changes before the doctrine of the separation of church and state, which we take for granted today, was adopted.

What happened to alter the Puritans' concept of government? Much of the shift can be attributed to the thinking, writings, and persuasive actions of Thomas Jefferson, that well-traveled, well-read, ***cosmopolitan*** (POL) man of the late 1700s and early 1800s. Jefferson's desire to incorporate the ideal of religious freedom into the laws of the United

States accounts almost fully for our country's early switch to a nonbiased government. He had a vision of a nation whose affairs would, under the Constitution, be totally separate from the institutions of religion.

In 1777, Jefferson, who sat in the General Assembly of the State of Virginia, wrote a bill calling for the establishment of religious freedom in Virginia. Because of the varying opinions held by lawmakers at that time, we can only imagine that the debate before passage must have been heated. However, the bill was adopted in the Virginia Assembly on January 16, 1786, and subsequently served as a model for the First Amendment of the Constitution.

Freedom of religion is now guaranteed to all Americans under this amendment, which states that "Congress shall make no law respecting an establishment of religion or prohibiting the free exercise thereof." The guarantee, however, has proven to be a controversial one throughout U.S. history. In the 1800s, for instance, the government forbade the Mormons certain of their beliefs because such beliefs were in conflict with United States laws. During the same period, some Native American tribes were also denied their religious practices.

Since that time, the separation of church and state in America has evolved and changed. Americans have seen the legality of individual religious freedoms continue to be tested and the Constitution of the United States reinterpreted in numerous ways. Even today, though, the disputes go on: public displays of religious material and the legality of prayer in school settings stir up strong feelings in every community. It appears that "freedom of religion," like religion itself, will never mean the same thing to everyone.

1. John Winthrop seemed to envision the Puritan settlement in America as
   A. a commune in which everyone could do as he or she pleased.
   B. a settlement in which various religions could live together peacefully, but each have its own community government.
   C. *a nation in which religious and civic authorities would share power.*
   D. a temporary shelter from the religious persecutions of Europe.

2. The man who finally accomplished the passage of the Virginia Act for Establishing Religious Freedom in Virginia in 1786 was
   A. *Thomas Jefferson.*
   B. John Winthrop.
   C. James Madison.
   D. an unknown Mormon Elder.

3. Which of the following brings up the issue of separation of church and state?
   A. Saying a prayer in a high school football huddle
   B. Using the words "Under God" in the Pledge of Allegiance
   C. Setting up an outdoor Christmas scene showing the birth of Jesus
   D. Reading passages from the Koran aloud in a class
   E. *All of the above*

Exercise VI. Drawing on your knowledge of roots and words in context, read the following selection and define the *italicized* words. Note that the prefix *tri* means "three" and that the prefix *mega* means "great, large." If you cannot figure out the meaning of the words on your own, look them up in a dictionary. *Answers will vary by student.*

Pompeii, Caesar, Crassus. Antony, Lepidus, Octavian. Six of the Roman Empire's greatest generals and politicians joined forces to create two *triumvirates*. The first *triumvirate* was formed by Gnaeus Pompeii, Julius Caesar, and Marcus Crassus. The three joined in 60 B.C. to share control of the Roman Empire. The second *triumvirate* was formed by Marc Antony, Marcus Lepidus, and Octavian. Both groupings lead to the eventual control by a single ruler, as two of the men in each trio were killed in military battles. Under the rule of both *triumvirates*, the boundaries of the Empire were extended throughout Europe, Asia, and Africa, and Rome, with its diverse population and unprecedented size, became a true *megalopolis*.

UNIT FIFTEEN

DIC/DICT
Latin **DICERE, DICTUM** "to say, to order"

DICTATE (dik´ tāt) (1) *v.* To speak aloud in order that one's words may be copied or recorded
(2) *v.* To give an order; to make necessary
(1) Regina *dictated* a letter for her secretary.
(2) Our current circumstances *dictate* that we conserve money and resources.
syn: demand   *ant:* allow

MALEDICTION (mal ə dik´ shən) *n.* A recital of words intended to harm; a curse
L. male, "badly," + dicere = *speaking badly (of one)*
To Claudia, Leo's angry words were practically a *malediction*.

BENEDICTION (ben ə dik´ shən) *n.* A blessing
L. bene, "well," + dictum = *to speak well*
A local rabbi started the ceremony by giving a *benediction* to the audience.

LOC/LOQU
Latin **LOQUI, LOCUTUS** "to speak"

LOCUTION (lō kyōō´ shən) *n.* Style or action of speaking
Nothing about Francis' careful *locution* betrayed his nervousness.

ELOQUENT (el´ ə kwənt) *adj.* Powerful and expressive
Brenda composed an *eloquent* tribute for her younger sister's wedding.
syn: articulate   *ant:* unclear

COLLOQUIAL (kə lō´ kwē əl) *adj.* Of or related to informal speech; conversational
L. con, "together," + loqui = *to speak together*
When the residents of Stoneville were interviewed on television, they dropped some of their *colloquial* expressions in favor of more formal language.
syn: idiomatic

▥ *Another name for "word choice" is diction. An author's diction can convey the tone of a work.*

▥ *Ventriloquism, literally meaning "wind-speech," is the art of "throwing your voice."*

VOCA
Latin **VOCARE, VOCATUM** "to call"

EVOCATIVE (ē väk´ ə tiv) *adj.* Calling forth a vivid image or impression
L. e, "out of," + vocatum = *to call out (of memory or mind)*
The novel features an *evocative* description of a lakeside town in Michigan.
syn: suggestive

EQUIVOCATE (ē kwiv´ ə kāt) *v.* To use misleading or confusing language
L. equi, "equal," + vocere = *to say (two things) equally*
Because Shonda felt it her duty never to *equivocate* to a client, she made a point of discussing both sides of every problem.
syn: evade

ADVOCATE (ad´ və kāt) (1) *v.* To argue in favor of
       (ad´ və kət) (2) *n.* Someone who argues for
L. ad, "toward," + vocere = *to call to toward*
(1) The senator plans to *advocate* capital punishment for those convicted of murder.
syn: recommend   *ant:* oppose
(2) As an *advocate* of careful financial planning, I cannot go along with your plan to invest in a bubble-gum factory.
syn: supporter   *ant:* enemy

CLAM/CLAIM
From Latin **CLAMARE, CLAMATUM** "to shout or call"

EXCLAMATORY (eks klam´ ə tôr ē) *adj.* Having a forceful, excited, or emotional tone
L. ex, "out of," + clamare = *shouting out*
Mr. Litt is famous for the *exclamatory* style of his speeches.

DECLAIM (dē klām´) *v.* To speak loudly and with feeling
L. de, "down from," + clamare = *to shout down from*
Martin *declaimed* upon the subject of tax hikes until he was blue in the face.

CLAMOROUS (klam´ ər əs) *adj.* Characterized by a loud noise or outcry
The pianist entered the auditorium to *clamorous* applause.
syn: ear-splitting   *ant:* quiet

The crowd was so CLAMOROUS that the GLAMOROUS singer could not be heard.

Ⅲ *Your* vocation *is your job or profession; your* avocation *is a hobby or a pleasure activity.*

Ⅲ *To* declaim *can mean either "to make a formal speech," as in the sentence "Young George will* declaim *upon the topic in the rhetorical exhibition," or "to rant," as in the sentence at left.*

EXERCISES - UNIT FIFTEEN

Exercise I. Complete the sentence in a way that shows you understand the meaning of the italicized vocabulary word. *Answers will vary by student.*

1. The *eloquent* tribute by Lorenzo to his former teacher made her feel...

2. During the *benediction*, the speaker told the graduating class that...

3. As an *advocate* of stricter environmental laws, Janet believes...

4. When asked whether he had witnessed the crime, the man *equivocated*, saying...

5. Nicole spoke *colloquial* English only when she was...

6. Philip's financial difficulties *dictate* that he...

7. The *evocative* lyrics about the canals of old Venice made me ...

8. The young debater's flawless *locution* made him seem...

9. The movie's hero utters a *malediction* against his enemy when...

10. The *clamorous* shrieking of the monkeys high above caused the explorers to ...

11. Preacher Bell's *exclamatory* sermons often prompted members of the congregation to...

12. Anton angrily *declaimed* about the score he had received, but the judges...

Exercise II. Fill in the blank with the best word from the choices below. One word will not be used.

colloquial   locution   malediction   evocative   dictate

1. If you have ever learned a foreign language, you know that ___colloquial___ speech is very different from formal, correct speech.

2. The hockey league let the temperature of the ice ___dictate___ the game schedule.

3. While I think the writer has some talent, his language is not ___evocative___ of the places he describes.

4. Having uttered a powerful ___malediction___ against his evil uncle, the prince departed the kingdom.

Fill in the blank with the best word from the choices below. One word will not be used.

equivocate   eloquent   advocate   benediction   locution

5.   Carla gave a(n) ___*eloquent*___ speech in honor of the bride, and everyone applauded.

6.   Miss Hutchins, my second-grade teacher, never allowed her students to ___*equivocate*___; she wanted a yes-or-no answer.

7.   Tommy's ___*locution*___ reveals that he is a trained Shakespearean actor.

8.   While composing the ___*benediction*___ for the ceremony, the leader thought carefully about what he wanted to say.

Fill in the blank with the best word from the choices below. One word will not be used.

equivocate   clamorous   advocate   declaim   exclamatory

9.   I am a(n) ___*advocate*___ of child safety, but I also think children should be given some freedom.

10. Lisa heard the ___*clamorous*___ wailing of the babies long before she reached the nursery.

11. On what dull topic must we listen to the professor ___*declaim*___ today?

12. The radio host's remarks always struck me as overly energetic and ___*exclamatory*___.

Exercise III. Choose the set of words that best completes the sentence.

1.   Although Graham is a both an excellent scholar and a(n) _____ speaker, he always tries to _____ praise he receives.
     A. evocative; equivocate
     B. eloquent; deflect
     C. colloquial; dictate
     D. evocative; declaim

2.   Because I believe that the population increase _____ that we build more houses, I am a(n) _____ of development in this area.
     A. declaims; malediction
     B. dictates; advocate
     C. equivocates; locution
     D. declaims; advocate

3. The poet _____ endlessly upon the harm that technology has done to the world, but I find his words and images beautifully _____ of the places he describes.
    A. equivocates; clamorous
    B. advocates; exclamatory
    C. advocates; colloquial
    D. *declaims; evocative*

4. In a rather _____ letter expressing his outrage, Martin did not _____ about who was to blame for the crime in the city.
    A. exclamatory; advocate
    B. *exclamatory; equivocate*
    C. eloquent; declaim
    D. colloquial; advocate

5. When the singer visiting the small town smiled and uttered a(n) _____ phrase common only in that region, the audience burst into _____ cheers.
    A. exclamatory; evocative
    B. eloquent; colloquial
    C. *colloquial; clamorous*
    D. evocative; eloquent

Exercise IV. Complete the sentence by drawing an inference about the *italicized* word from its context.

Answers will vary by student.

1. If Cynthia directs a *malediction* at Jake, we can assume that she…

2. If you *advocate* being constantly prepared, and you see me with an umbrella, you will probably tell me…

3. When writing an evaluation of the actor's *locution*, the acting coach will probably consider things like…

Exercise V. Fill in the blank with the word from the Unit that best completes the sentence, using the root we supply as a clue. Then, answer the questions that follow the paragraphs.

Reversing Global Warming

According to the Environmental Protection Agency, the Earth's surface temperature has risen one degree Fahrenheit over the past century. This gradual process is called global warming, and although one degree in a hundred years does not seem like much to most people, many scientists and environmentalists warn that it can be devastating to the earth's environment. For this reason, they **advocate** (VOC) major reforms in the practices that lead to global warming. Man, they say, would be naïve to believe that his own activities have no impact on the environment.

Global warming is not, by nature, a bad thing. In fact, it is a necessity for life on earth. The sun's energy sets Earth's climate in motion; Earth, in turn, radiates energy back into space. Greenhouse gases such as methane and carbon dioxide trap some of that energy, helping to keep the earth warm. If this natural process, called the greenhouse effect, did not occur, the earth would become too cold to sustain life. In recent years, however, the greenhouse effect has been unusually strong, causing dramatic shifts in climate and weather worldwide. What could explain this sudden change in a previously balanced system?

A growing body of scientists now believes that since the Industrial Revolution of the nineteenth century, human activities have significantly contributed to the rise in temperature of the atmosphere. The International Panel on Climate Control (IPCC) has stated that human beings have a discernible influence on the earth's climate and that the warming trend is probably not entirely natural in origin. The Panel points out that increased use of motor vehicles, heating and cooling of houses, operation of factories, and harvesting of timber all add to the gases that alter the chemical composition of the earth's atmosphere.

Scientists have reason to be concerned. As warmer temperatures cause ice and snow in the Arctic Ocean to melt, global sea levels begin to rise. In addition, atmospheric changes are increasing the annual amount of rainfall worldwide. The overabundance of water results in the submersion of coastal lands once used to support food crops or residential areas. And the loss of these lands is not the only disturbing pattern. Climatic changes resulting from global warming can lead to the extinction of various forms of life on earth, and the composition of the air human beings breathe is

being affected in ways that may contribute to the ill health of millions.

If human beings are indeed responsible for global warming, they must take measures to reverse the damage to the planet. The replacement of gas-burning motor vehicles by electric ones would be a step in the right direction, as would stricter preservation of the world's rain forests. But these small steps may ultimately not be sufficient given the rapid growth of industry and population. For this reason, many environmentalists believe that the precarious ecological situation __*dictates*__ (DIC) that humankind change many of its attitudes and practices, regardless of politics and economics.

1. Which of the following human activities contributes to global warming?
   A. Operating factories
   B. Driving gas-fueled cars
   C. Driving gas-fueled trucks
   D. Heating and cooling houses
   E. All the above

2. What is the purpose of the third paragraph?
   A. To explain how global warming is a harmful natural phenomenon
   B. To show that global warming is made harmful by human beings
   C. To argue that global warming is a social and economic dilemma
   D. To reevaluate the validity of the claims of environmentalists

3. Judging by the passage, what can we assume would happen if human activities did not have an impact on the greenhouse effect?
   A. The earth would get colder.
   B. The earth would get hotter at a faster rate.
   C. The earth's temperature would remain more constant.
   D. There would be a second Ice Age.

Exercise VI. Drawing on your knowledge of roots and words in context, read the following selection and define the *italicized* words. Note that the prefix *ab* means "away from," *re* means "back," and *ir* is a form of *in*, meaning "not." If you cannot figure out the meaning of the words on your own, look them up in a dictionary.

Answers will vary by student.

On December 10, 1936, King Edward VII of England became the first, and only, British monarch to voluntarily *abdicate* the throne. Edward gave up his crown after falling in love with a married woman, Wallis Warfield Simpson. Edward unsuccessfully attempted to win over the rest of the royal family in support of his love. When he realized the cause was lost, Edward gave up his claim to the throne, proclaiming, "I, Edward, do hereby declare my *irrevocable* determination to renounce the throne for myself and my descendants." After his retirement, he accepted the title of Governor of the Bahamas.

UNIT SIXTEEN

CRUX
Latin **CRUX** "cross"

EXCRUCIATING (eks krōō´ shē āt ing) *adj.* Extremely painful; agonizing
L. ex, "out of," + crux = *from the cross*
Min was forced to sit through an *excruciating* series of piano recitals.
syn: unbearable   *ant:* pleasant

CRUX (kruks) *n.* The most important or decisive point
The *crux* of the matter is the difference between children and adults.
syn: essence   *ant:* extra

CRUCIAL (krōō´shəl) *adj.* Extremely necessary; essential
Good study skills are often *crucial* to success in high school and college.

DOL
Latin **DOLERE** "to feel pain, to be grieved"

INDOLENT (in´ də lənt) *adj.* Lazy; averse to work
L. in, "not," + dolere = *feeling no pain*
Being of a somewhat *indolent* character, Paige was not inclined to take on extra jobs.
syn: listless   *ant:* robust

DOLEFUL (dōl´ fəl) *adj.* Sad; mournful
You can tell by Greg's constantly *doleful* expression that he has a gloomy nature.
syn: depressed   *ant:* cheerful

DOLOROUS (dōl´ ər əs) *adj.* Mournful; gloomy
The *dolorous* chanting of the monks was made even sadder by the steady, gray rain.
syn: bleak   *ant:* uplifting

▥ Crucifixion, *or execution by cross, was fairly common in ancient Rome. Thus the word* crux, *"cross," became associated with torture. Later,* crux *came to mean "a crossroads, a decision point"—something that determines what is most important. From this second meaning, we get our words "crux" and "crucial."*

▥ *How do you think we got a word meaning "lazy" from a root that means "to feel no pain"?*

ACRI
Latin **ACER** "sharp"

ACERBIC (əs ûr´ bik) *adj.* Harsh and biting in tone
L. acerbus (from acer)   *sharp, biting*
Cal's *acerbic* reply to the reporters earned him a reputation as an ill-tempered man.
syn: sharp   *ant*: bland

ACRID (ak´ rid) *adj.* Stinging or biting in odor or taste;
     harsh; irritating
The *acrid* fumes that filled the office soon had us
coughing and rubbing our eyes.

ACK!!! RID us of that ACRID odor!!

ACRIMONIOUS (ak rə mō´ nē əs) *adj.* Exhibiting harsh
     sharpness in speech or mood
L. acer, "sharp," + mony, "quality of" = *having a sharp, bitter quality*
The *acrimonious* debate between the two candidates did not help either one in the polls.
syn: bitter   *ant*: civil

EXACERBATE (eg za´ sər bāt) *v.* To make worse or more severe
L. ex, "out of," + acer = *to make (something) harsher out of*
Mira's comments, which were supposed to be helpful, only *exacerbated* Shelley's problem.
syn: aggravate   *ant*: ease

FERV
Latin **FERVERE** "to boil, be warm"

FERVENT (fûr´ vənt) *adj.* Passionately excited or enthusiastic
Grace, a *fervent* supporter of the Democratic Party, cheered enthusiastically when her favorite candidate was elected.
syn: fiery   *ant*: indifferent

FERVOR (fûr´ vər) *n.* Emotional excitement; heated enthusiasm
The *fervor* Ron displays when discussing cars lets me know he'll make a great mechanic.
syn: eagerness   *ant*: apathy

EFFERVESCENT (ef ər ves´ ənt) *adj.* Highly spirited; animated
L. ex, "out of," + fervere = *boiling out of*
The young horse had a cheerful, almost *effervescent* character.
syn: bubbly   *ant*: lifeless

▥ *Why do you think some-one in high spirits would be called effervescent?*

EXERCISES - UNIT SIXTEEN

Exercise I. Complete the sentence in a way that shows you understand the meaning of the italicized vocabulary word.   *Answers will vary by student.*

1.   The *effervescent* cheering of the fans in the stands caused the team to…

2.   The *doleful* mood that Luke has been in recently is a result of…

3.   When the *acrid* city air blew into our faces, we…

4.   The mayor wanted to get to the *crux* of the matter because…

5.   On one particularly *excruciating* exam day, I felt…

6.   The *indolent* nature of the two sisters was apparent when they…

7.   We could tell the argument had become *acrimonious* when…

8.   Trisha's desire to see the band was obviously *fervent*, because…

9.   When headquarters told the astronaut that fixing the part was *crucial*, he…

10.   If you find that the medicine *exacerbates* your problem, you should…

11.   When Cynthia heard the *dolorous* song, she felt…

12.   Lulu was *acerbic* when she spoke to Adam because…

Exercise II. Fill in the blank with the best word from the choices below. One word will not be used.

indolent   dolorous   crux   excruciating   fervent

1.   The ___*crux*___ of the problem is that my friend and I fight constantly.

2.   I know that, being ___*indolent*___, you just want to sit around and eat potato chips, but you should get some exercise instead.

3.   It is George's ___*fervent*___ hope that his favorite actress will answer his letters.

4.   The critic found the film so awful that just sitting through it caused her ___*excruciating*___ pain.

Fill in the blank with the best word from the choices below. One word will not be used.

     acrimonious   doleful   acrid   acerbic   exacerbate

5.   The gloomy colors of the room seemed to ___*exacerbate*___ the sadness that Joyce felt.

6.   The twins had a really ___*acrimonious*___ fight, and they hurt each other's feelings deeply.

7.   When Francoise heard the ___*doleful*___ whistle of a lonely train, she began to weep.

8.   If you are less ___*acerbic*___ to the children when they ask questions, they won't think of you as grumpy.

Fill in the blank with the best word from the choices below. One word will not be used.

     effervescent   crux   fervor   acrid   crucial

9.   Hilda was amazed at the ___*fervor*___ Tim displayed when talking about his beloved model trains.

10.   It is ___*crucial*___ that we reach the trapped skiers before the temperature drops.

11.   If the fumes of the factory are so ___*acrid*___ that your eyes burn, you should stay out of that area.

12.   I felt such ___*effervescent*___ happiness that I seemed to be floating instead of walking.

Exercise III. Choose the set of words that best completes the sentence.

1.   In his typical sarcastic, _____ way, Robin sneered that I was too _____ to accomplish any work at all.
    A. effervescent; acrid
    B. *acerbic; indolent*
    C. doleful; acerbic
    D. excruciating; crucial

2.   Michael knew it was _____ for him to pull himself out of his _____ mood, so he tried to think of happy things.
    A. acrid; fervor
    B. indolent; crux
    C. excruciating; fervor
    D. *crucial; dolorous*

3.   I am afraid that Clark's wish to own a motorcycle is so _____ that seeing any vehicle — car, bicycle
     or otherwise — will only _____ the problem.
     A.   fervent; exacerbate
     B.   acerbic; indolent
     C.   effervescent; exacerbate
     D.   acrid; exacerbate

4.   Sherry switched rapidly from the bitterness of the _____ screaming match to the _____
     cheerfulness she needed for the party.
     A.   acrimonious; effervescent
     B.   dolorous; excruciating
     C.   fervent; acrid
     D.   acrid; doleful

5.   The _____ of our city's problem is the _____, polluted air caused by factories, cars, and resi-
     dents burning trash.
     A.   fervor; acrid
     B.   fervor; fervent
     C.   crux; acrid
     D.   crux; effervescent

Exercise IV. Complete the sentence by drawing an inference about the *italicized* word from its context.

   Answers will vary by student.

1.   If Laurie displays a *fervor* for her religion, Pete can assume her experiences in her church have been…

2.   The children seem rather *indolent* to their grandmother; she might suspect the children's parents have
     not…

3.   Jill's attempt to settle an argument between Steve and Dave *exacerbates* the argument, so Jill will
     probably…

**Exercise V. Fill in the blank with the word from the Unit that best completes the sentence, using the
     root we supply as a clue. Then, answer the questions that follow the paragraphs.**

   In addition to being the coldest place on Earth, Antarctica is the world's largest desert. With an average of two inches of precipitation per year in its central regions, Antarctica remains covered by ice only because the little snowfall each year never thaws. Due to these barren conditions, Antarctica has never supported human beings or large land animals. The birds and seals that spend their time on Antarctica's coasts depend on the surrounding waters for sustenance. Encompassing Antarctica are seas rich in plankton (microscopic marine algae), which serve as food for tiny, shrimp-like krill. Krill, in turn, are a ___*crucial*___(CRUC) food source for the whales, seals, and penguins of Antarctica.

   The abundance of fur seals, elephant seals, and various types of whales has brought international attention to Antarctica. Between 1784 and 1822, Europeans hunted millions of fur seals for their skins along Antarctic coasts. The skins were prepared for trade with China, which was extremely profitable at the time. Whale hunters, who sold whale oil for use as lamp fuel, ventured south during this period, but were unable to capture the fast-moving Antarctic rorquals. Instead, they hunted elephant seals and rendered them into oil as a substitution for whale oil. At times, when the elephant seals became scarce, hunters also targeted penguins for their oil. The penguin population, however, was not devastated to the same degree as the seal colonies were. Commercial interests in seals during this era left the fur and elephant seal populations near extinction. By the end of the nineteenth century, the seal population was recovering, but the presence of hunters searching for whales near Antarctica again resulted in the slaughter of elephant seals for their oil.

Advancements in whaling technology brought whalers back to the shores of Antarctica in 1904. Faster catch boats and explosive harpoons allowed whalers to finally capture the humpback and blue whales they sought in the South as well as exhaust the supply of whales in Northern waters. England and Norway dominated the industry initially, but Japanese hunters took the lead in the 1930's. By 1965, hunters had killed hundreds of thousands of whales off the shores of Antarctica, and the whale population was less than 10% of its original size. The International Whaling Commission imposed a moratorium on commercial whaling in 1968, in an attempt to salvage the whale population. The restriction remains in place today.

Although fur and elephant seals have significantly increased their numbers since the last surge of hunting in the 1890's, there remains no notable increase in the whale population after nearly forty years of protection. The effect of the decreased numbers of whales on the Antarctic ecosystem is still under investigation.

1. What would be an appropriate title for this passage?
    A. Antarctica's Imbalanced Ecosystem
    B. The Exploration of Antarctica
    C. The Hunting of Antarctica's Seals and Whales
    D. The World's Vastest Desert

2. From its use in the sentence, "Whale hunters…ventured south during this period, but were unable to capture the fast-moving Antarctic rorquals," what do you think a "rorqual" is?
    A. a whale
    B. a seal
    C. a penguin
    D. an iceberg

3. What animal(s) did whalers hunt to produce a substitution for whale oil?
    A. elephant seals
    B. elephant seals and penguins
    C. fur seals and penguins
    D. fur seals

4. What is krill, and why is it important in the Antarctic waters?
    A. Krill is a marine algae, and is important because sea creatures depend on it.
    B. Krill is a type of whale that has been a main target for hunters in Antarctica.
    C. Krill is a crustacean that marine algae depend on for food.
    D. Krill is a shrimp-like food source for animals in the Antarctic waters.

Exercise VI. Drawing on your knowledge of roots and words in context, read the following selection and define the *italicized* words. Note that the prefix *con* means "with." If you **cannot** figure out the meaning of the words on your own, look them up in a dictionary.

   Answers will vary by student.

Mrs. Hanson had always been a *fervid* supporter of the Democratic party. In addition to working long hours putting up flyers and attending rallies during the week, she spent many Saturdays doing extra work for her local chapter. When she was forced to give up her job campaigning for the Party to take care of her ailing husband, her fellow-campaigners missed her very much. When Mrs. Hanson's husband died, many local Democrats came to express their *condolences* to their bereaved coworker.

UNIT SEVENTEEN

PUT
Latin **PUTARE, PUTATUM** "to think"

IMPUTE (im pyōōt´) *v.* To assign blame or responsibility for
L. in, "on, against" + putare = *to think against*
The car's manufacturer *imputed* the steering problems to faulty tires.
syn: attribute   *ant:* vindicate

DISPUTE (dis pyōōt´)   (1) *v.* To disagree with
                           (2) *n.* A disagreement or argument
L. dis, "apart," + putare = *to think apart*
(1) Lisa *disputed* my claim that she was always late; in
     fact, she said, she was usually early.
syn: deny   *ant:* agree
(2) The city council was divided by the *dispute* over
     sales taxes.
syn: argument   *ant:* agreement

CLUTE'S DISPUTE over falling leaves was solved with a chainsaw.

DISREPUTABLE (dis rep´ yōō tə bəl) *adj.* Not respectable;
          having a bad reputation
L. dis, "bad," + re, "again," + putare = *thought badly of
again and again*
The *disreputable* doctor allowed his patients to go for months or years without
treatment.
syn: notorious   *ant:* respectable

III *A reputation* (re, "over," + putare) *is an opinion of you that people have after thinking over your qualities. If you are disreputable, you have a bad reputation.*

NOTA
Latin **NOTARE, NOTATUM** "to note"

CONNOTATION (kän ə tā´ shən) *n.* An image or idea associated with a word
L. con, "together with," + notatum = *noted with*
I fully understand the negative *connotation* of the word you used to describe me.
syn: overtone

DENOTATION (dē nō tā´ shən) *n.* The dictionary definition of a word
L. de, "down," + notare = *noted from*
In order to grasp the *denotation* of the word, I looked it up in several dictionaries.

ANNOTATE (an´ ə tāt) *v.* To explain or discuss through a note
L. ad, "towards," + notare = *noted upon*
The difficult book would have attracted more readers if the author had decided
to *annotate* it.

RATIO
Latin **RATIO** "reason"

IRRATIONAL (ir rash´ən əl) *adj.*   Not based on reason or logic
L. in, "not," + ratio = *(having) no reason*
As a child, Christopher was teased for his *irrational* fear of water.
syn: illogical   *ant*: reasonable, rational

RATIONALE (rash ə nal´) *n.* A reason for doing something; explanation
What *rationale* does the author provide for designing the book this way?

RATIONALIZE (rash´ ən əl īz) *v.* Justify; give reason for
I tried my best to *rationalize* spending so much money on one piece of furniture.
syn: excuse

SCI
Latin **SCIRE** "to know"

CONSCIENTIOUS (kän shē en´ shəs) *adj.* Diligent and careful
L. com, "with," + scire = *in accordance with knowledge*
Rebecca was a *conscientious* student and a leader in several school clubs.
                    ant: careless

UNCONSCIONABLE (un kän´ shə nə bəl) *adj.*   Not obeying moral laws;
   unscrupulous
L. un, "not," + con, "with," + scire = *not in accordance with knowledge*
The current administration's repeal of environmental laws has been called *unconscionable* by many naturalists.
                    ant: principled

PRESCIENT (presh´ ənt) *adj.* Showing knowledge of events before they happen
L. pre, "in advance," + scire = *to know in advance*
The baseball coach made some decisions that now seem amazingly *prescient*.
syn: far-sighted   *ant*: rash

III *The verb* rationalize *has a more negative meaning than its noun counterpart,* rationale. *A rationale is simply a reason, while* rationalize *means "to make an excuse."*

EXERCISES - UNIT SEVENTEEN

Exercise I. Complete the sentence in a way that shows you understand the meaning of the italicized vocabulary word. *Answers will vary by student.*

1. The historian decided to *annotate* the chapters in his newest book because...

2. Celeste is a *conscientious* student, so she is sure to...

3. Because of her connection to some *disreputable* businessmen, Naya...

4. The *denotation* of the term that you gave was incorrect because...

5. The only *rationale* I could provide for jumping out of the plane was...

6. If Noah *imputes* Herman's mistake to bad manners, it is because he thinks...

7. My grandmother, hearing about the tornado on the radio, took the *prescient* step of...

8. Sometimes people can be offended by the *connotation* of a word even when...

9. Having worked hard on the project, Lara decided to *dispute*...

10. Norah says that, because other people need food and medicine, it is *unconscionable* to...

11. The man *rationalized* his involvement in the candy store robbery by...

12. It seems *irrational* of Harriet to get angry at Morgan for...

Exercise II. Fill in the blank with the best word from the choices below. One word will not be used.

conscientious   rationale   annotated   dispute   prescient

1. A(n) __*annotated*__ chapter explained some of the medical terms used in the book.

2. My __*rationale*__ for cutting class and going to the beach was that it was the first really warm day of the year.

3. Fred insisted that the property line ended at the tree, but his neighbor might __*dispute*__ the claim.

4. Many people later called the police chief __*prescient*__ for beefing up the force prior to the major crime wave.

Fill in the blank with the best word from the choices below. One word will not be used.

disreputable   irrational   impute   annotate   conscientious

5.   My father believed that even a(n) ___*disreputable*___ man could redeem himself by doing good deeds.

6.   Natasha feels that if she is ___*conscientious*___ about doing her job, she will make very few mistakes.

7.   Some citizens ___*impute*___ the rougher winds in our town to the destruction of trees that served as wind blocks.

8.   Although I know my fear of spiders is ___*irrational*___, I can't go near them.

Fill in the blank with the best word from the choices below. One word will not be used.

impute   connotation   rationalize   denotation   unconscionable

9.   The dictionary's ___*denotation*___ of the word surprised me, since I'd always thought it had a different meaning.

10.   It can be easy to ___*rationalize*___ a bad decision if you do not think about all the consequences.

11.   It was **unconscionable** of Dina to injure a man with her car and then leave the scene.

12.   If you know the ___*connotation*___ of that term, you know it is actually a compliment.

Exercise III. Choose the set of words that best completes the sentence.

1.   You may _____ the claim that the quarterback meant to throw the ball too far, but in light of the play's success, the decision seems very _____.
     A. dispute; prescient
     B. rationalize; conscientious
     C. impute; rationale
     D. dispute; irrational

2.   How can Julian possibly _____ using a word with such a negative _____ to describe this great man?
     A. impute; rationale
     B. dispute; repute
     C. rationalize; connotation
     D. connotation; denotation

3. The historian explains his _____ for writing the book both in the introduction and in the chapters he _____ with footnotes.
    A. connotation; disputes
    B. rationale; disputes
    C. rationale; annotates
    D. denotation; imputes

4. One benefit of being a(n) _____ student is never having to do something as _____ as cheating.
    A. prescient; rationale
    B. irrational; disreputable
    C. conscientious; unconscionable
    D. conscientious; dispute

5. While I think it is rather _____ to look to the stars for answers, some people _____ all their troubles to the constellations.
    A. irrational; impute
    B. conscientious; rationalize
    C. prescient; impute
    D. unconscionable; rationalize

Exercise IV. Complete the sentence by drawing an inference about the *italicized* word from its context.

   Answers will vary by student.

1. If an expert on the stock market is often called *prescient*, his predictions about financial affairs probably…

2. If Sally worries about the *connotation* of a particular word that she used in describing a coworker, she is probably afraid that…

3. If a medical study *imputes* an illness to a popular medicine, the doctors in the study will probably…

Exercise V. Fill in the blank with the word from the Unit that best completes the sentence, using the root we supply as a clue. Then, answer the questions that follow the paragraphs.

A Leader in the New South

It is difficult to __*dispute*__ (PUT) the claim that Booker T. Washington was the most influential African-American educator of the late 19th and early 20th centuries. In addition to his contributions to educational theory and practice, Washington had a great impact on race relations in the newly emancipated South and was a leading figure in black public affairs from 1895 until his death in 1915. His success is all the more admirable when one considers that he started life as a slave on a Virginia plantation and slowly worked his way into politics, finally rising to international prominence with his founding of the Tuskegee Institute in Alabama (1881).

Washington was a dedicated supporter of industrial education among African-Americans. His support of the Tuskegee Institute placed him in a public spotlight, allowing him to address the subject of racial tensions in general. Washington worked hard to convince Southern white employers and governors that Tuskegee offered an education that would keep blacks "down on the farm" and in the trade industries. To prospective Northern donors, particularly new self-made millionaires such as Rockefeller and Carnegie, he made a promise to train students in the ways of the Protestant work ethic. To blacks living with little hope of future success, Washington offered the __*rationale*__ (RAT) that industrial education could be a means of escape from poverty; it would lead, he told them, to self-employment, land ownership, and even small business ownership. His charismatic nature allowed him to procure some money from the federal government, but it was Northern donations that made the Tuskegee Institute the best-supported black educational institution in the country. His most famous speech was "The Atlanta Compromise Address," delivered before the Cotton States Exposition in 1895. The central theme of his speech was racial tolerance: Washington issued an appeal to whites to encourage black progress in economics and education, while remaining "separate fingers" on the hand that builds society.

Washington tried to translate his own personal successes into black advancement through sponsorship of civil rights suits, serving on the boards of Fisk and Howard Universities, and directing charitable contributions to these and other black colleges. Through various speaking tours and personal communications, he tried to gain equal public educational opportunities for African-Americans as well as to reduce racial violence. Unfortunately, these efforts were generally unsuccessful, and the year of Washington's death marked the beginning of the Great Migration from the rural South to the urban North.

It became apparent at this time that whites had gained control over Southern institutions after the Civil War, and that they had never wanted equal rights for African-Americans. Many blacks began to turn to the more radical leaders of the time, including William Trotter and W.E.B. DuBois. Nevertheless, Booker T. Washington is still believed to have been a __*prescient*__ (SCI) thinker: he had an immense effect on the minds of post-war Southerners, and his theories continue to have an impact today.

1. Which of the following best describes the author's intentions in the writing of this essay?
    A. to explain the differences between Booker T. Washington and other prominent African-American leaders at the time, such as W.E.B. DuBois and William Trotter
    B. to argue that the Tuskegee Institute was the greatest college of the 19th century
    C. to explain how Booker T. Washington rose to international prominence
    D. *to describe the lasting contributions Booker T. Washington made towards American civil rights*

2. The author discusses all of the following as reasons for Washington's international popularity EXCEPT
    A. the publication of his autobiography.
    B. the creation of the Tuskegee Institute.
    C. *his speeches and fundraising efforts.*
    D. his ability to bridge a racial gap between Southern whites and newly emancipated African-American slaves.

3. According to the passage, which of the following famous phrases or statements would Booker T. Washington probably use?
    A. *"Separate but equal"*
    B. "Peace, love, and happiness"
    C. "By any means necessary"
    D. "Life is a lesson I never want to learn."

4. Washington's image of the races being separate fingers on the same hand is an important one. Which of the following statements most accurately describes the meaning of the symbol?
    A. All races originated in the same place, but have since become quite fond of one another.
    B. If races are completely integrated, more can be accomplished.
    C. *All races have to work together to accomplish something, and the motivation for all is the same.*
    D. Some races are far superior to others.

Exercise VI. Drawing on your knowledge of roots and words in context, read the following selection and define the *italicized* words. Note that the prefix *re* means "again," and *omni* means "all." If you cannot figure out the meaning of the words on your own, look them up in a dictionary. *Answers will vary by student.*

The poet and artist William Blake was *reputed* to sing his poems aloud before writing them down. His friends and family compared his singing to that of the ancient bard, who also sang and wrote poems. In fact, Blake writes of the bard in one of his poems, referring to the writer-musician as *omniscient*. However, there is no evidence showing that Blake envisioned himself, like the bard, as all-knowing and all-powerful.

UNIT EIGHTEEN

AES
Greek **AESTHESIS** "feeling, perception"

The Greek word aesthesis means both "sensory perception"—the ability to feel heat or cold, for instance—and "perception of the beautiful."

AESTHETIC (es thet´ ik) *adj.*   Having to do with beauty or order
The statue has an *aesthetic* value that will last far beyond our own time.
syn: artistic

ANESTHETIC (an es thet´ ik) *n.* A substance which causes loss of feeling
G. an, "without," + aesthesis = *without feeling*
The doctor administered an *anesthetic* before operating on the patient's foot.

PATH
Greek **PATHEIN** "to feel"

APATHETIC (ap ə thet´ ik) *adj.* Not interested; having no strong emotion towards
G. a, "not," + pathein = *having no feeling*
The speaker tried to rally the crowd, but most of the people present were *apathetic*.
syn: indifferent

EMPATHY (em´ pə thē) *n.* Sharing of another's emotions
G. em, "inside," + pathos = *feel from inside*
Nelly was divided between feeling *empathy* for her boss and concern about her own future at the company.
syn: compassion   *ant:* opposition

PATHOS (pā´ thōs) *n.* Power of evoking great sadness or sympathy
The sheer *pathos* of the opera's final scene left the audience in tears.
syn: pitifulness

ANTIPATHY (an tip´ ə thē) *adj.* Hostility or hatred
G. anti, "against," + pathein = *feeling against*
The fans' *antipathy* for the coach increased when he lost the game.
syn: dislike   *ant:* sympathy

AUNTIE PATTY felt strong ANTIPATHY towards anyone who cheated at cards.

SENS/SENT
Latin SENTIRE, SENSUM "to feel, to be aware"

SENTIENT (sen´ shənt) *adj.* Conscious; aware
Do you think there are other *sentient* beings in the universe?
ant: unaware

SENTINEL (sen´ ti nəl) *n.* One who watches or guards
L. literally, *one being aware*
George was posted as *sentinel* over the camp.

SENTIMENT (sen´ tə mənt) *n.* A feeling about something
Although Vinnie expressed his sincere love for Sandra, she did not return the *sentiment*.
syn: attitude

PRESENTIMENT (prē zent´ ə mənt) *n.* A feeling about something before it happens
L. pre, "before," + sentire = *feeling before*
I had an uneasy *presentiment* about the party that evening.
syn: foreboding

> ▥ *A sentiment can be a simple feeling about something; to be sentimental is to be too emotional.*

TANG/TACT
Latin TANGERE, TACTUM "to touch"

TANGIBLE (tan´ jə bəl) *adj.* Able to be grasped or perceived
The rewards of volunteering may not be as *tangible* as a new car or a new house, but they are just as real.
syn: concrete   *ant*: abstract

TACTILE (tak´ tīl) *adj.* Pertaining to touch
The poet uses *tactile* imagery to give his reader the feeling of rough boards and damp sand.

INTACT (in takt´) *adj.* Unbroken; whole
L. in, "not," + tactum = *not touched*
Amazingly, the vase was *intact* even after rolling to the bottom of the hill.
syn: unharmed

EXERCISES - UNIT EIGHTEEN

Exercise I. Complete the sentence in a way that shows you understand the meaning of the italicized word.

Answers will vary by student.

1. When my sister lost her job, I felt *empathy* for her because...

2. The teacher encouraged *tactile* interaction between the children and their environment by...

3. Once the *anesthetic* was administered, Dan started to...

4. The *sentinel* at the military base looked for...

5. Although he had once expressed *antipathy* for his stepfather, Owen now...

6. The *presentiment* I had about the meeting caused me to...

7. Justin thought the rug had *aesthetic* appeal, but Jeremy thought...

8. Some people argue that humans are the only *sentient* beings because...

9. Alvin found that the results of his hours at the gym were *tangible* when...

10. The *pathos* of the scene in which the girl kneels beside her kitten made me...

11. When he found that the priceless figurine was *intact*, the collector...

12. The *sentiment* expressed by most of the excited fans at the game was...

13. Nicole was *apathetic* about the idea of the dance until...

Exercise II. Fill in the blank with the best word from the choices below. One word will not be used.

 pathos   anesthetic   tangible   tactile   sentient

1. The ___**pathos**___ of Chris' situation certainly made me feel pity for him.

2. As ___**sentient**___ beings, we have the power to understand the world around us.

3. The changes the new boss made in the company were both abstract and ___**tangible**___.

4. We explore our environment not only through vision and hearing, but in a(n) ___**tactile**___ way.

Fill in the blank with the best word from the choices below. One word will not be used.

sentinel   empathy   anesthetic   intact   presentiment

5.   Although I had a(n) __*presentiment*__ of disaster, I stepped onto the plane.

6.   Because Gina has suffered greatly, she can feel __*empathy*__ for other people in pain.

7.   My arm was bruised but __*intact*__, and I walked off the ski slope basically unhurt.

8.   The drug had a(n) __*anesthetic*__ effect, and Del began to lose feeling in his leg.

Fill in the blank with the best word from the choices below. One word will not be used.

sentinel   aesthetic   tactile   apathetic   antipathy

9.   Drew is anything but __*apathetic*__ about democracy; he has voted in every local, state, and national election for ten years.

10.   The __*sentinel*__ began to shout that he saw the enemy's torches in the distance.

11.   The __*antipathy*__ I had for Kip only increased when he started insulting my friends.

12.   Even though the beautiful old piano doesn't work, it has a(n) __*aesthetic*__ value.

Exercise III. Choose the set of words that best completes the sentence.

1.   William felt some _____ for the artist whose paintings were destroyed, though he had never agreed with her _____ principles.
     A.   presentiment; anesthetic
     B.   antipathy; sentient
     C.   pathos; anesthetic
     D.   empathy; aesthetic

2.   As _____ beings, we are aware of others' emotions; this awareness allows us to feel the _____ of a great tragedy.
     A.   sentient; anesthetic
     B.   aesthetic; antipathy
     C.   sentient; pathos
     D.   tactile; presentiment

3.   The army came out of the first day of battle tired but _____, and posted a _____ to keep guard over the camp that night.
     A.   apathetic; pathos
     B.   intact; sentinel
     C.   sentient; sentiment
     D.   anesthetic; presentiment

4.   The only _____ reward I get from my job as a volunteer painter is a finished canvas, but the work also gives me _____ satisfaction.
      A.   tactile; sentient
      B.   anesthetic; tactile
      C.   **tangible; aesthetic**
      D.   sentient; anesthetic

5.   Although Sean had had a _____ that the day would go badly, he was not prepared for the _____ directed at him by his coworkers.
      A.   pathos; sentinel
      B.   sentinel; empathy
      C.   **presentiment; antipathy**
      D.   presentiment; sentinel

Exercise IV. Complete the sentence by drawing an inference about the *italicized* word from its context.

> ***Answers will vary by student.***

1.   If an architect complains that most modern buildings have no redeeming *aesthetic* value, he probably means that…

2.   When Virginia feels *empathy* for Eric, who has just been severely injured in a car accident, it is probably because…

3.   If Oliver explains to you that the rewards of gardening are *tangible*, he probably means that…

Exercise V. Fill in the blank with the word from the Unit that best completes the sentence, using the root we supply as a clue. Then, answer the questions that follow the paragraphs.

A Champion for Everyone

In 1981, out of deep ____**empathy**____ (PATH) for the many children who were too poor to afford adequate athletic training and equipment, three-time Olympic gold medalist Wilma Rudolph started the Wilma Rudolph Foundation. The purpose of the organization was to help underprivileged young athletes get the resources and assistance they needed to overcome the numerous obstacles that severe poverty and racism presented. Once again, Rudolph proved that she was firmly determined to reduce or eliminate these obstacles wherever she found them.

Wilma Rudolph had really been set on the path towards the Foundation when she was four years old. One of many children in an impoverished household, she was stricken with a debilitating disease that was later diagnosed as polio, and one of her legs became almost useless as a result. Nonetheless, with the help of her family, she was able to walk almost normally by the age of nine and was soon playing basketball with her brother. In high school, she had to struggle to gain recognition for her talent as an athlete. The segregated school system allocated few of its resources to all-black schools, and Rudolph's school had little equipment or money to participate in competitions. Luckily, Rudolph's talent came to the attention of Ed Temple, the track coach at Tennessee State University. Rudolph eventually became a track star at Tennessee State, and then an Olympic medalist on a team coached by Temple. Her gold medal was a ____**tangible**____ (TANG) reward for all of her struggles over the years.

Rudolph was welcomed home from the Olympics to Clarksville, Tennessee, with an enormous parade. At the time, her town was still mostly segregated, and the governor of Tennessee, an ardent segregationist himself, indicated that blacks and whites would be separated during the parade. Rudolph declared that she would not be a part of a segregated celebration. While this stance no doubt earned her the ____**antipathy**____ (PATH) of many devotees of the color line, she stood firm, and by her determination furthered the advancement of civil rights in America. In fact, the parade was the first integrated event in Clarksville's history.

Her own experiences with poverty and racial injustice made Wilma Rudolph all the more determined not only to succeed herself, but also to help others succeed. Her primary objective after the Olympics was not stardom, but nurturing athletic talent where it might otherwise not have the opportunity to develop. After all, she herself had been helped along by people who saw how much she loved to run and knew how to turn her passion into a career.

Rudolph's former coach, Ed Temple, once said about her that she had done more for the United States than she had ever been compensated for. Surely the athletes who grew up in awe of Rudolph's talent and grace would echo this ___**sentiment**___ (SENT).

1. Why does the author mention the Wilma Rudolph Foundation?
    A. as a way of demonstrating Wilma Rudolph's desire to help others overcome poverty
    B. as a way of proving that Rudolph was strongly opposed to racism
    C. as a way of explaining Rudolph's influence on later athletes
    D. as a way of making clear Rudolph's determination to learn to walk

2. Why, according to the author, was Rudolph's success unlikely to occur?
    A. because Rudolph and Temple were from different parts of the country
    B. because Rudolph came from a poor school with few resources
    C. because Rudolph was involved in an accident at an early age
    D. because Rudolph was unaware of the opportunities awaiting athletes

3. What did Rudolph's gold medal provide for her?
    A. a reason to continue as an athlete
    B. a symbol of the evils of segregation
    C. a solid, real prize for her long struggle
    D. a solution to the problem of poverty

Exercise VI. Drawing on your knowledge of roots and words in context, read the following selection and define the *italicized* words. Note that the suffix *as* (from *ad*) means "towards." If you cannot figure out the meaning of the words on your own, look them up in a dictionary.

Answers will vary by student.

Esther looked out her window when she heard the *pathetic* cries of a baby bird abandoned in its nest. She noticed that the bird was sad, alone, and clearly too small to fly, so she decided to keep it company. Raising her window, she began to sing a little song, urging the bird to take heart. The tiny bird, as if giving its *assent*, began to chirp with delight.

UNIT NINETEEN

QUIS
Latin **QUAERERE, QUISITUM** "ask, seek, demand"

INQUISITIVE (in kwiz´ ə tiv) *adj.* Curious; asking many questions

L. in, "in," + quisitum = *seeking into*
Being a somewhat *inquisitive* child, Marian was inclined to ask questions that were difficult to answer.

                                      ant: uninterested

ACQUISITIVE (ə kwiz´ ə tiv) *adj.* Seeking to get things; greedy
L. ad, "toward," + quisitum = *seeking towards*
The property was purchased by an *acquisitive* businesswoman who already owned much of the surrounding land.
syn: demanding   *ant*: generous

REQUISITION (re kwə zish´ən) (1) *n.* Act of ordering or demanding something
                              (2) *v.* to make a request or demand
L. re, "again," + quisitum = *demand again*
(1) The army issued another *requisition* for backup troops and food supplies.
(2) The lieutenant had *requisitioned* several horses for backup troops and food supplies.

SPOND/SPOUSE
Latin **SPONDERE, SPONSUM** "pledge, show support for"

ESPOUSE (e spouz´) *v.* To support; pledge support to
Although he *espouses* the right of free speech, Kenneth doesn't like to listen to me.
syn: advocate   *ant*: criticize

CORRESPOND (kôr ə spänd´) *v.* To be similar to; compare to
L. con, "together with," + spondere = *support back with*
The scientist showed us how a bone in the dolphin *corresponded* to a bone in the human.
syn: match   *ant*: differ

DESPONDENT (dəs pän´ dənt) *adj.* Lacking all hope
L. de, "down," + spondere = *having pledged away (hope)*
When Leah lost her job and then her house, she became *despondent*.
syn: despairing   *ant*: joyful

▥ English took the word "espouse" from French, which dropped the "n" from sponsum *and added an "e" to its beginning.*

The DESPONDENT CORRESPONDENT could not get an interview with the actress.

ROG
Latin **ROGARE, ROGATUM** "to ask, demand"

INTERROGATE (in ter´ ə gāt) *v.* To formally question
L. inter, "between," + rogare = *question between regular intervals*
Though the detectives formally *interrogated* the butler twice, his story remained the same.
syn: grill

DEROGATORY (dər räg´ ə tôr ē) *adj.* Insulting; degrading
L. de, "down," + rogare = *seeking to take down*
Boomer and Buzz, hosts of the morning talk show, were criticized for making *derogatory* comments about a certain political figure.
syn: belittling   *ant*: complimentary

ARROGANT (ar´ ə gənt) *adj.* Excessively proud; haughty
L. ad, "towards," + rogare = *demanding from*
It was *arrogant* of Philip to suggest that he could tutor the rest of the class in math.
syn: conceited   *ant*: humble

ABROGATE (ab´rə gāt) *v.* To cancel; to repeal
L. ab, "from," + rogare = *to seek away from*
If one country decides to *abrogate* the treaty, the other country will start a war.
syn: abolish   *ant*: ratify

PREC
Latin **PREX, PRECIS** "prayer"

PRECARIOUS (prē kâr´ ē əs) *adj.* Threatened or unsafe
L. literally, *praying (for one's safety)*
Cindy was in a *precarious* position on the old bridge; no matter which way she stepped, it looked like she would fall.
syn: risky   *ant*: safe

IMPRECATION (im pri kā´ shən) *v.* A curse
L. in, "against," + precis = *a prayer against*
The holy man called down an *imprecation* upon the murderous king.
                              ant: blessing

DEPRECATE (dep´ rə kāt) *v.* To show disapproval of
L. de, "off, away" + precis = *to pray away from*
Your novel may not be perfect, but you shouldn't *deprecate* the work you have done so far.
syn: belittle   *ant*: praise

Ⅲ *To deprecate is literally to "avert disaster by praying to someone"—in a way, "to apologize." From its apologetic overtones, we get the meaning "put down (oneself)" or just "put down."*

EXERCISES - UNIT NINETEEN

Exercise I. Complete the sentence in a way that shows you understand the meaning of the italicized vocabulary word. *Answers will vary by student.*

1.   If the company issues a *requisition* for pens and paper,...

2.   Although I know you are *despondent* now, eventually you will be...

3.   When Pierre was *interrogated* about the warehouse fire, he...

4.   The strong *imprecation* you directed at me made me feel...

5.   The manager of the office was in a *precarious* position at work because...

6.   When our *inquisitive* puppy, Junie, saw the snapping turtle, she...

7.   It was clear that the oil tycoon was growing more *acquisitive* as the years went by because he...

8.   If you *espouse* principles of kindness and love, you will...

9.   Olivia found the speaker's remarks *derogatory*, but Pam thought...

10.   If one of the parties in the contract decides to *abrogate*, the other party will...

11.   I thought that many things in the new country would *correspond* to things in my homeland, but...

12.   Before you *deprecate* the job of a teacher, you should know that...

13.   The twins' *arrogant* behavior often made their friends...

Exercise II. Fill in the blank with the best word from the choices below. One word will not be used.

inquisitive   despondent   abrogate   precarious   interrogate

1.   Although some people feel it is dangerous to be too __*inquisitive*__, others think you should seek knowledge constantly.

2.   The priest found himself in a(n) __*precarious*__ position; he did not know whom to trust, but he could not keep the information secret.

3.   When France chose to __*abrogate*__ the treaty with Britain, the British were outraged.

4.   I am afraid that if the police decide to __*interrogate*__ me, I will not be able to answer their questions.

Fill in the blank with the best word from the choices below. One word will not be used.

imprecations   despondent   requisition   espouse   acquisitive

5.   If you would stop screaming __*imprecations*__, maybe we could talk like civilized people.

6.   When Trina learned that she would not graduate, she became __*despondent*__.

7.   The relief organization needed to __*requisition*__ more food for the hungry refugees.

8.   Marty claims to __*espouse*__ the founding principles of an independent political party.

Fill in the blank with the best word from the choices below. One word will not be used.

deprecate   acquisitive   interrogate   arrogant   derogatory

9.   Because of her rather __*acquisitive*__ nature, Jill tends to accumulate goods and possessions.

10. In what many considered a(n) __*arrogant*__ gesture, the senator refused to meet with any members of the committee.

11. I demanded an apology for a comment I thought was __*derogatory*__.

12. It was Fred's habit to __*deprecate*__ the achievements of his noble family because he didn't want to seem vain.

Exercise III. Choose the set of words that best completes the sentence.

1.   If you keep making such _____ comments about your little sister, you'll make her sad or even _____.
     A. inquisitive; derogatory
     B. derogatory; despondent
     C. inquisitive; precarious
     D. precarious; despondent

2.   The country was in a(n) _____ position, unsure whether to _____ the treaty or not.
     A. despondent; correspond
     B. acquisitive; espouse
     C. precarious; abrogate
     D. derogatory; deprecate

3.   It is hard to see how someone as _____ and conceited as Mr. Thorpe could _____ the principles of modesty and kindness.
     A. despondent; abrogate
     B. arrogant; espouse
     C. acquisitive; deprecate
     D. arrogant; correspond

4. While doing extra research, the _____ student discovered that words in one language _____ to the words in another.
    A. **inquisitive; corresponded**
    B. despondent; interrogated
    C. precarious; deprecated
    D. inquisitive; espoused

5. If you _____ Danny, you can be sure he will get back at you with some unrepeatable _____.
    A. correspond; prerequisite
    B. **deprecate; imprecation**
    C. abrogate; imprecation
    D. interrogate; acquisitive

Exercise IV. Complete the sentence by drawing an inference about the *italicized* word from its context.

   Answers will vary by student.

1. If someone described Mark as *acquisitive*, you might expect to see Mark constantly...

2. When a nation *abrogates* a treaty, another nation under the treaty will probably...

3. If someone who knows about a crime is *interrogated*, he or she will probably...

Exercise V. Fill in the blank with the word from the Unit that best completes the sentence, using the root we supply as a clue. Then, answer the questions that follow the paragraphs.

Who Was Shakespeare?

In recent years, a controversial theory has gained a following among Shakespearean scholars: that Edward de Vere, 17th Earl of Oxford and a learned court insider during the Elizabethan period, was actually the author of the plays and sonnets generally attributed to William Shakespeare. People who ___*espouse*___ (SPOUS) this view claim that "Shakespeare" was merely a clever pen name, and that de Vere assumed the identity of a commoner in order to publish his politically scandalous writings. Their case was first argued by Charlton Ogburn in his book *The Mysterious William Shakespeare.*

Ogburn laid out a comprehensive argument based mainly on the Stratfordian Shakespeare's lineage and education. This Shakespeare was the son of a tradesman, and evidence that he received formal instruction is inconclusive. History records that he was a sometime actor and occasional real-estate investor. His death seemed to go unnoticed, and was not marked by the notices in the press that one would expect for a great writer.

Furthermore, the Stratfordian's will mentions no writings, and there is no evidence that he ever owned a book. How, supporters of Ogburn inquire, can anyone reconcile the brilliance of the writings with such an obscure existence?

The life of Edward de Vere, however, really does seem to ___*correspond*___ (SPOND) to the range of knowledge reflected in the work of Shakespeare. De Vere came from a wealthy family and was England's highest-ranking earl. He was a poet, an adventurer, and a court regular; his extensive education and knowledge of the world would have prepared him exceedingly well for a second career as a playwright and sonneteer. In addition, the de Vere theorists have a ready motive for their author-in-disguise: he wanted to publish politically sensitive material, but would have been exiled or worse for doing so openly.

Ogburn's book made an immediate impact on scholars of English literature. It set the stage for various debates and mock trials, including one before three U.S. Supreme Court justices. Although the final "trial" ended with a decision in favor of the original Shakespeare, the controversy continues. Those who believe de Vere was Shakespeare must accept an elaborate hoax and a conspiracy of silence, while those who side with the man from Stratford must lean heavily on the miraculous power of human creativity.

1. Which of the following is NOT an argument of Ogburn's supporters?
   A. The real Shakespeare came from an obscure family, so he would have been unlikely to gain literary fame.
   B. ***Shakespeare and de Vere were partners in a "conspiracy of silence."***
   C. De Vere could not express himself freely, so he used an alias to publish his opinions.
   D. De Vere, unlike Shakespeare, was clearly a very educated man.

2. What is the purpose of the first paragraph?
   A. ***to explain the identity controversy surrounding Shakespeare and de Vere, and to note the function of Ogburn's book in the controversy***
   B. to argue that de Vere took "Shakespeare" as a pen name and assumed the identity of a commoner
   C. to describe the Shakespearean scholars who are involved in the de Vere controversy
   D. to explain why de Vere is a likely candidate for the real Shakespeare

3. What is the purpose of the sentence, "His death seemed to go unnoticed and was not marked by the notices in the press that one would expect for a great writer"?
   A. The author is explaining the relationship of Edward de Vere to Shakespeare.
   B. ***The author is explaining why one might not believe that the stratfordian Shakespeare actually wrote the famous plays and sonnets.***
   C. The author is explaining why de Vere might have been disguised as a playwright.
   D. The author is explaining why Shakespeare came from a middle-class family.

Exercise VI. Drawing on your knowledge of roots and words in context, read the following selection and define the *italicized* words. Note that the prefix *pre* means "before." If you cannot figure out the meaning of the words on your own, look them up in a dictionary.

    Answers will vary by student.

    The entire courtroom was so moved by the woman's story that it came as no surprise when the prosecutor had a change of heart. The woman's tale of loss and sorrow, coupled with the testimony of her daughter, clearly made any attempt at argument by the prosecution pointless. At a press conference following the hearing, the prosecutor said that it was his *prerogative* to drop the charges, since he was the one who brought them up in the first place.

UNIT TWENTY

MON
Latin **MONERE, MONITUM** "to warn"

ADMONITION (ad mə nish´ ən) *n.* Gentle scolding
L. ad, "toward," + monitum = *warning toward*
The judge released me with the *admonition* to stay away from people who got me into trouble.
syn: chiding

PREMONITION (pre mə nish´ən) *n.* A vision; a warning of something before it
   happens
L. pre, "before," + monitum = *warning before*
Although I had a *premonition* that the day would go badly, I stepped onto the plane.
syn: foreboding, forewarning

CONSIL
Latin   **CONCILIARE,** "bring together"
         CONSILIUM, "advice"

🏛 *The Latin word* conciliare *means "to call together, to bring to assembly." In Rome, a group that was called together (the Senate, for instance) could provide* consilium, *or advice, to a leader.*

COUNSEL (koun´ səl) (1) *v.* To advise; make a suggestion to
                        (2) *n.* Advice
(1) The farmer's brother *counseled* him to sell the farm and move to the city.
syn: encourage   *ant:* discourage
(2) The lottery winners will seek the *counsel* of a lawyer before revealing their
   identities.

CONCILIATORY (kən sil´ ē ə tôr ē) *adj.* Intended to lessen another's anger
In a *conciliatory* gesture, Judith offered to give her medal to her opponent.
syn: appeasing   *ant:* defiant, aggressive

RECONCILE (rek´ ən sīl) *v.* To bring back into agreement
L. re, "back," + consiliare = *to bring back together*
Dawn tried to *reconcile* two of her friends who were fighting.
syn: harmonize   *ant:* upset

The warring CROCODILES finally RECONCILED.

CAUT
Latin **CAVEO, CAUTUM** "to be careful"

PRECAUTION (prē kô´ shən) *n.* An action taken against danger ahead of time
L. pre, "before," cautum = *be careful before*
I have never been in an accident, but I always wear my seatbelt as a *precaution.*

CAUTIOUS (kô´ shəs) *adj.* Careful not to get into danger
After a series of major financial scandals, investors are usually more *cautious.*
syn: prudent

CAUTIONARY (kô´ shən e rē) *adj.* Intended to serve as a warning
The minister told us a *cautionary* tale about the dangers of vanity.

SUAD
Latin **SUADERE, SUASUM** "advise"

DISSUADE (di swād´) *v.* To convince one not to do something
L. dis, "not," + suasum = *advise not to*
No matter how I tried, I could not *dissuade* Vince from going into the haunted house.
syn: discourage   *ant:* persuade

PERSUASION (pər swā´ zhen) *n.* Habit or type
I certainly know people who love all kinds of sports, although I am not of that *persuasion.*
syn: camp

▥ *The phrase* caveat emptor *means "let the buyer beware"; a caveat is a warning.*

▥ *At one time, the noun* persuasion *meant "the religion one is persuaded to believe in." Eventually, it lost its connection with religion and came to mean "type" or "kind."*

EXERCISES - UNIT TWENTY

Exercise I. Complete the sentence in a way that shows you understand the meaning of the italicized vocabulary word. *Answers will vary by student.*

1.   If Frank, whom Lisa does not trust, *counsels* Lisa to take a job, Lisa will probably…

2.   Connie, who was usually on the *cautious* side, surprised us by…

3.   One *admonition* that mothers often issue to their children is…

4.   When Irene had an unpleasant *premonition* about the trip, she decided to…

5.   In order to *reconcile* my sisters, who had been fighting for months, I…

6.   As a *precaution*, the firemen always…

7.   As a *conciliatory* act towards his political opponent, Governor Hodges…

8.   When small children hear a *cautionary* tale, they usually…

9.   The only way to *dissuade* a very stubborn person from doing something is to…

10.   Most of the people at the party were of the *persuasion* that likes classical music, but some…

Exercise II. Fill in the blank with the best word from the choices below. One word will not be used.

       admonition   dissuade   conciliatory   counsel

1.   I could not __**dissuade**__ Parker from entering the beauty contest, no matter how hard I tried.

2.   Do you think Peter's gift of his favorite toy to KC was a(n) __**conciliatory**__ act, meant to win back his brother's favor?

3.   Having given Lionel a(n) __**admonition**__ about being more careful, the teacher let him go.

Fill in the blank with the best word from the choices below. One word will not be used.

       precaution   counsel   premonition   cautious   reconcile

4.   If you __**counsel**__ Reed to seek help with his homework, he will probably take your advice.

5.   I had a terrible __**premonition**__, and decided to stay home instead of going to work.

6.   Be __**cautious**__ when it comes to your personal finances; try to save money.

7.   If you can __**reconcile**__ these two opinions, which are so different, I will be amazed.

Fill in the blank with the best word from the choices below. One word will not be used.

cautionary   persuasion   precaution   reconcile

8.   As a ___*precaution*___, always wear a helmet when you ride your bike.

9.   I am of the ___*persuasion*___ that likes to stay in and read books; my sister is the sort of person who likes to go to parties and movies.

10. A ___*cautionary*___ story about not judging people made all of us rethink our values.

Exercise III. Choose the set of words that best completes the sentence.

1.   If you are of the _____ that does not like to take _____, be prepared for bad things to happen.
     A. *persuasion; precautions*
     B. precaution; persuasions
     C. admonition; counsel
     D. counsel; admonition

2.   The _____ tale warned that if you don't try to _____ yourself with your enemies, everyone will suffer.
     A. conciliatory; dissuade
     B. *cautionary; reconcile*
     C. cautious; dissuade
     D. cautionary; counsel

3.   Although I cannot _____ you from getting back at the man who took your money, at least I can _____ you to be extremely careful.
     A. reconcile; dissuade
     B. cautionary; counsel
     C. dissuade; reconcile
     D. *dissuade; counsel*

4.   Instead of being _____ after our fight, Hannah gave me a(n) _____ about not being so bossy.
     A. cautionary; counsel
     B. *conciliatory; admonition*
     C. cautious; persuasion
     D. conciliatory; persuasion

5.   After I had a terrible _____ about a car crash, I started being more _____ on the roads.
     A. admonition; cautious
     B. premonition; counseled
     C. *premonition; cautious*
     D. admonition; conciliatory

Exercise IV. Complete the sentence by drawing an inference about the *italicized* word from its context.

Answers will vary by student.

1.   If your best friend *counsels* you to accept an offer, you will likely…

2.   If you try to *reconcile* two friends, another will assume they have been…

3.   A person usually gives an *admonition* to another person who has…

Exercise V. Fill in the blank with the word from the Unit that best completes the sentence, using the root we supply as a clue. Then, answer the questions that follow the paragraphs.

Inspired by her own difficulties, Eleanor Roosevelt carried on a long heritage of political activism. Her early education helped to foster a deep interest in social causes, especially those involving women, the poor, and all under-privileged people. She was an early member of the National Consumer's League, striving for improvement of working conditions for women. As a young woman of 21, against the __*cautionary*__ (CAUT) advice of her future mother-in-law, she became the wife of Franklin Delano Roosevelt. This marriage was to provide Eleanor with her greatest opportunities to bring about political change.

During the First World War, Eleanor was active in many volunteer organizations, including the Red Cross. Upon her husband's appointment to President Woodrow Wilson's Cabinet, Eleanor took advantage of the opportunity to lead the cause for more social reform and became more involved in politics herself. After Franklin Roosevelt lost his bid for the Vice Presidency in 1920 and was diagnosed with polio, Eleanor threw herself into efforts for the causes she supported, including women's independence. She held office in the League of Women Voters and the Democratic Committee of New York. She spent considerable time campaigning for Democratic candidates across New York State, even, at one point, trying to __*dissuade*__ (SUAD) people from voting for her Republican cousin Theodore Roosevelt, Jr., in his bid for governor.

She championed the cause of women workers, African-Americans, writers, scholars, artists, and actors. The first white resident in Washington, D.C. to join the NAACP, she resigned from the Daughters of the American Revolution when the organization failed to grant membership to renowned black singer Marian Anderson. She fought against racial discrimination, comparing segregation and racism in America to fascism abroad. Her crusade for an end to discrimination even made her a target of the Ku Klux Klan.

During World War II, Eleanor visited troops in Europe and held a position in the Office of Civil Defense. She was an independent journalist, a gifted public speaker, a magazine columnist, and a beloved radio personality. However, she and Franklin could not __*reconcile*__ (CONSIL) their opposing views about a woman's place in society. At her husband's request, she reluctantly gave up many of the activities in which she was involved.

After Franklin's death, Eleanor remained loyal to liberal causes that were not always supported by the governing administration. However, President Harry Truman, despite the fact that her views differed from his own, appointed Roosevelt to the post of US Representative to the United Nations. She led the Human Rights Commission for five years, and later, by appointment of President John Kennedy, led the National Commission on the Status of Women.

1.   Which of the following conclusions can be drawn from the article?
     A.   Franklin Roosevelt approved of all his wife's activities.
     B.   Eleanor Roosevelt was an advocate of social causes.
     C.   Studying makes a woman a political candidate.
     D.   Presidents don't like women to be in politics.

2.   Which of the following would be the best title for the passage?
     A.   Eleanor Roosevelt's Change of Heart
     B.   A President's Wife Speaks Out
     C.   A First Lady's Activism
     D.   How to Succeed as a Woman

3.   From the passage, we can infer that Eleanor Roosevelt did not want to surrender her leadership roles in certain organizations because
     A.   she thought that staying at home would be dangerous.
     B.   she enjoyed working for her husband.
     C.   she was jealous of her husband's position.
     D.   she thought she would lose the power to accomplish her goals.

Exercise VI. Drawing on your knowledge of roots and words in context, read the following selection and define the *italicized* words. Note that the prefix *in* means "not." If you cannot figure out the meaning of the words on your own, look them up in a dictionary.

Answers will vary by student.

The city commissioners met at the conference room to discuss the building of a new statue for the park. After deciding on a *monument* in honor of prisoners of war, they invited Mr. Hadley into the room. Mr. Hadley was an environmental consultant who came to discuss the pollution risks of construction near the park's lake. He had often warned the commissioners not to be *incautious* when it came to the environment.

UNIT TWENTY-ONE

GUST
Latin **GUSTUS**, "taste"

GUSTO (gəs´ tō) *n.* Enthusiastic enjoyment
The hungry children dug into the delicious spaghetti with great *gusto*.
syn: relish   *ant*: dislike

GUSTATORY (gəs´ tə tôr ē) *adj.* Having to do with the sense of taste
Gene thanked the waiter for the best *gustatory* experience of his life.

SIP, SAP
Latin **SAPERE**, "to taste"

INSIPID (in si´ pəd) *adj.* Dull; uninteresting
Latin in, "not," + sapere = *having no taste*
Wendy quickly tired of her sister's *insipid* conversation.
syn: colorless   *ant*: intriguing

SAPIENT (sā´ pē ənt) *adj.* Having knowledge; wise
Human beings have long thought themselves the only *sapient* beings on planet Earth.
syn: conscious   *ant*: unthinking

AV
Latin **AVERE**, "to crave, to desire"

AVID (a´ vəd) *adj.* Enthusiastic; eager
Stan was such an *avid* fan of the team that he called in sick rather than miss the big game.
syn: devoted   *ant*: uninterested

AVARICE (a´ və rəs) *n.* Desire for wealth; greed
Nelson's *avarice* led him to make risky decisions on behalf of the company.

▥ *The verb* sapere *was often used by Roman authors to mean not only "taste," but "have good taste" or "be wise." This second meaning is the one that has influenced our English words. It is why, for example, the name of the species to which human beings belong is Homo Sapiens—literally, "Wise Men."*

BIB
Latin **BIBERE**, "to drink"

IMBIBE (im bīb´) *v.* Drink; soak up
in, "into," + bibere= *drink in*
Spanish merchants, having *imbibed* the culture of their Middle Eastern trading partners, brought new customs back to Spain.
syn: absorb

BIBULOUS (bi´ byə ləs) *adj.* Drunken
When I asked how the party was going, Chuck gave me a *bibulous* grin.

GLUT
Latin **GLUTTIRE**, "to devour"

GLUT (glət) *n.* Too much of something; oversupply
The *glut* of similar-sounding songs on the radio station drove listeners to change the channel.

GLUTTON (glə´ tən) *n.* One who wants or takes too much (especially food or drink)
Anyone who eats as much turkey as Sheila did is a *glutton* in my opinion.

PALAT
Latin **PALATUM**, "palate"

PALATE (pa´ lət) *n.* Taste or liking
Although many people like the music of Mozart, it does not suit my *palate*.
syn: appetite

PALATABLE (pa´ lə tə bəl) *adj.* Acceptable; satisfactory
I found the actor's impressions *palatable*, but I wouldn't recommend him for any awards.
syn: tolerable   *ant:* unbearable

▥ *Medieval religious beliefs stated that seven sins were particularly terrible; these were therefore called the seven "deadly sins." Avarice and gluttony are two; the others are wrath, sloth, pride, lust and envy.*

EXERCISES - UNIT TWENTY-ONE

Exercise I. Complete the sentence in a way that shows you understand the meaning of the italicized vocabulary word.   *Answers will vary by student.*

1.   Edgar believes that *sapient* organisms may inhabit another planet because...

2.   Because Doreen did not find the professor's ideas *palatable*, she...

3.   Tired of the *insipid* dialogue in the movie, I decided to...

4.   Marc was an *avid* chess player, so he often...

5.   Frank calls the Hot Dog Shack "a *gustatory* house of horrors" because...

6.   My aunt has a very limited *palate* when it comes to sports; she only...

7.   When the freshwater plants *imbibed* the salty water, they...

8.   Because of the *glut* of crops on the market this season, the farmers saw...

9.   When asked about her years abroad, Samantha remembers *bibulous* evenings that often ended in...

10.   Terrence ate his lima beans with unusual *gusto* because...

11.   If I let my little brother, a *glutton* by nature, see the new box of cookies...

12.   The *avarice* displayed by the leaders of the country is especially shameful because...

Exercise II. Fill in the blank with the best word from the choices below. One word will not be used.

   gusto   avarice   sapient   avid   bibulous

1.   The personal ad read, "Looking for another ___*avid*___ golfer to share many hours on the golf course."

2.   Jay is a(n) ___*bibulous*___ fellow who can often be found cheerfully ordering a round of drinks for a group of complete strangers.

3.   Lisa found few friends who matched her intellectual ability, and often despaired of ever coming across anyone ___*sapient*___.

4.   After the pep talk, the basketball players went back to their work with new ___*gusto*___.

Fill in the blank with the best word from the choices below. One word will not be used.

glut   imbibe   palatable   gustatory   insipid

5. I remember so much about Paris—the sights, the sounds, and especially the ___*gustatory*___ plea-
    sures.

6. The hiring manager complained that a _____*glut*_____ of workers made it difficult to find jobs
    for everyone.

7. Imagine my surprise when my date turned out to be exciting and intelligent rather than a(n)
    ____*insipid*____ drone.

8. Because of television, citizens of one country may now _____*imbibe*_____ freely of the cultures of
    another.

Fill in the blank with the best word from the choices below. One word will not be used.

sapient   glutton   palate   avarice   palatable

9. The most important vow a monk takes involves giving up the pleasures of the world, so Brother
    John's ____*avarice*____ was confusing to everyone.

10. Are the candidates' speeches ____*palatable*____ to you, or do you find them disagreeable?

11. I was horrified to hear the mistress of the orphanage call the rail-thin child a ____*glutton*____.

12. Teresa traveled the world to develop her ____*palate*____ and see what she liked.

Exercise III. Choose the set of words that best completes the sentence.

1. Shonda, a(n) _____ reader since childhood, devoured the author's new book with great
    _____.
    A. palatable; gusto
    B. avid; avarice
    C. gustatory; glut
    D. avid; gusto

2. The count promises _____ delights and _____ hilarity at his next
    grand party.
    A. bibulous; sapient
    B. gustatory; bibulous
    C. palatable; sapient
    D. gustatory; insipid

3.   The student soon outgrew her teacher, and refused to _____ any more of his _____ _____ and uninspiring philosophy.
        A. glut; palatable
        B. imbibe; avid
        C. imbibe; insipid
        D. palate; avid

4.   Even the most _____ creatures among us must develop a(n) _____ for certain areas of knowledge.
        A. palatable; glut
        B. sapient; palate
        C. gluttonous; avarice
        D. bibulous; glutton

5.   Despite the _____ John displayed as a banker, he was not a(n) _____ at the dinner table.
        A. gusto; palate
        B. glut; avarice
        C. avarice; glutton
        D. palate; gusto

Exercise IV. Complete the sentence by drawing an inference about the italicized word from its context.

   Answers will vary by student.

1.   Faced with another day of *insipid* chatter in the lounge, Peter may choose to...

2.   If Semaj hears *bibulous* laughter coming from downstairs, he will probably assume that...

3.   Because I told Sarah's new boyfriend that she is an *avid* swimmer, he...

Exercise V. Fill in the blank with the word from the Unit that best completes the sentence, using the root we supply as a clue. Then answer the questions that follow.

A Career for Eternity

Much of Frank Sinatra's fame in both music and movies can be traced to one movie: "From Here to Eternity." Without this film, Sinatra would probably have disappeared from the spotlight.

In this 1953 picture set in pre-World War II Pearl Harbor, Sinatra plays Angelo Maggio, an underdog hero who resists the bullying of his sergeant (Ernest Borgnine)and eventually pays a terrible price. After several run-ins with the sergeant, whom he calls "Fatso," Maggio is arrested by military police for leaving his base without permission. His warden during the time of imprisonment is none other than Fatso, who spends several days beating him severely.

Maggio escapes the prison and, with his dying breath, reveals his murderer to his fellow-soldier and friend, Prewitt (played by Montgomery Clift). Prewitt avenges Maggio's murder in a way that further complicates the tragedy.

At the time "From Here to Eternity" came out, Sinatra's film and music careers both looked uncertain. He had been dropped from a major record label a year before; even ____**avid**____ (AV) fans now considered him a has-been. However, Sinatra pleaded with the film studio to give him a chance, even agreeing to accept a salary much lower than the going rate for actors of his stature, and he was chosen for the role.

The sincerity with which Sinatra delivered the role of Maggio won back old fans and earned him new ones. Maggio is an innocent character who likes to joke around, and who takes to life with great ___*gusto*___ (GUST) despite the war beginning all around him. In order to play the part, Sinatra had to understand the combination of childish vulnerability and stubborn heroism that makes the character so sympathetic.

Some critics of Sinatra's work in "From Here to Eternity" feel that he is playing a role not far removed from his own personality. Maggio, like Sinatra, is a funny, charming character of Italian extraction; some of his lines could have come straight out of Sinatra's comedy routines in Las Vegas. Other critics claim that the performance is overblown and melodramatic: Maggio, they say, goes from being irritatingly cheerful to unconvincingly pathethic (he dies in his best friend's arms).

Nevertheless, the film is now considered a classic. Despite the opinions of those who find Sinatra's acting work less than ___*palatable*___ (PALAT) or even unwatchable, moviegoers return to it again and again. It even won Sinatra an Oscar for Best Supporting Actor in 1954.

1. What can we infer would have happened if Sinatra had not landed the role in "From Here to Eternity"?
   A. His career as a singer would have reached new heights.
   B. **Neither his film nor his movie career would have advanced.**
   C. He would have started a new career as a director of movies.
   D. Moviegoers would have considered the film a classic.

2. How did the success of "From Here to Eternity" affect Sinatra's musical career?
   A. **It allowed him to stay in the spotlight and remain a musical artist as well as a film star.**
   B. It allowed Sinatra to sing beautifully throughout the film.
   C. It made Montgomery Clift, Sinatra's fellow-actor, decide to bankroll Sinatra's musical career.
   D. It allowed him to accept a below-average salary for his part in the film, and was therefore able to finance his next album.

3. Critics of the film say Maggio is too much like
   A. Montgomery Clift's character.
   B. an ordinary soldier.
   C. **Sinatra's stage persona.**
   D. "Fatso," the sergeant.

Exercise VI. Drawing on your knowledge of roots and words in context, read the following selection and define the *italicized* words.

Answers will vary by student.

Although the doctor had warned Kendra that the medicine might interfere with *gustation*, she was unprepared for what occurred. Dining became a chore, rather than a pleasure; even holidays were less enjoyable, because she was unable to really share the meals with her family. The *sapor* not only of food, but of life eluded her.

UNIT TWENTY-TWO

RANC
Latin RANCERE, "to stink"

RANCID (ran´ (t) səd) *adj.* Rotten; spoiled
After the power outage, we were forced to throw out three bottles of *rancid* milk.
syn: soured   *ant:* fresh

RANCOR (ran´ kər) *n.* Bitterness; hostility
The *rancor* between the two businesses was only deepened by disagreement over the new law.
syn: enmity   *ant:* friendliness

PUTR
Latin PUTRIS, "rotten"

PUTREFY (pyū´ trə fī) *v.* To rot; to decompose
The soldiers had to bury the bodies quickly so that they would not *putrefy* in the hot sun.

PUTRID (pyū´ trəd) *adj.*   Rotten; suggesting decomposition
The walls of the cave were covered with slime, and the air was filled with the stench of something *putrid*.
syn: rancid

▥ *The Spanish term* olla podrida, *which literally means "rotten pot," refers to a stew of meat and vegetables; it can also mean a mishmash of ideas.* Podrida *comes from* putris. *The French word* potpourri *is a translation of* olla podrida.

STAGN
Latin STAGNARE, "to stagnate, form a pool of standing water"

STAGNANT (stag´ nənt) *adj.* Unhealthy because of lack of movement
The *stagnant* air of the marsh was blamed for many illnesses.
syn: sluggish   *ant:* invigorating

STAGNATE (stag´ nāt) *v.* To stop moving or growing; to become unhealthy because of lack of movement
Marcia was afraid that she would *stagnate* in the unchallenging atmosphere of the office, but she actually found many opportunities to be creative.
syn: vegetate

▥ *While "stagnant" and "stagnate" literally apply to standing bodies of water, they may also be used figuratively. For example, a stagnant economy could use some stirring up.*

ODOR
Latin ODOR, "smell"

MALODOROUS (mal ō´ də rəs) *adj.* Foul-smelling
Latin malus, "bad" + olere= *bad-smelling*
Joelle could hardly bear to be in the room when her father opened the package of *malodorous* cheese.

ODORIFEROUS (ō də ri´ fə rəs) *adj.* Giving off an odor
L. odor + ferre, "to bear, carry" = *odor-bearing*
The herbal medicine smells strong because it is made of a combination of *odoriferous* plants.

OL
Latin OLERE, "to smell"

OLFACTORY (ä fak´ tə rē) *adj.* Having to do with the sense of smell
Latin olere + facere, "to make or do" = *ability to smell*
The *olfactory* ability of the average bloodhound makes it far better than a human being at following a scent.

REDOLENT (re´ də lənt) *adj.* Suggesting; carrying the hint of
Latin re, "back," + olere = *bringing the odor back*
I found the poet's essays *redolent* of the first days of the revolution.
syn: reminiscent

FET
Latin FETERE, "to stink"

FETID (fr´ təd) *adj.* Having an unpleasant smell
The *fetid* stench of rotting fish rose from the polluted stream.

> **III** Asafetida is a flavoring derived from a plant related to the carrot. Its name is combination of Persian aza, a name for a kind of tree-sap, and fetidus.

EXERCISES - UNIT TWENTY-TWO

Exercise I. Complete the sentence in a way that shows you understand the meaning of the italicized vocabulary word. *Answers will vary by student.*

1. I was surprised when Cheryl called the cookies *malodorous* because...

2. The pool in the deserted town started to *stagnate* when...

3. The atmosphere on the small town's main street was *redolent* of...

4. The ingredients in the compost pile started to *putrefy* after...

5. When the patient's *olfactory* nerve was injured, he...

6. Because the dangerous substance is both strongly colored and *odoriferous*...

7. The first camper who noticed the *rancid* vegetables...

8. Flies circled the *putrid* heap of scraps, making me feel...

9. The green, *stagnant* surface of the brook led me to believe that...

10. Trying to avoid the *rancor* that had filled their first meeting, the two groups...

11. Dawn believed that the *fetid* substance she had developed for her science fair project made the judges...

Exercise II. Fill in the blank with the best word from the choices below. One word will not be used.

putrefy   redolent   rancid   stagnate   malodorous

1. I was surprised when Suha claimed to find the odor of _____*rancid*_____ milk delightful.

2. Contrary to popular belief, pigs are not _____*malodorous*_____ creatures.

3. We hoped our fruit would last for months, but it began to spoil and _____*putrefy*_____ in the hot, moist air.

4. Brian was afraid that the water gathered in the sewer would _____*stagnate*_____ and breed disease.

Fill in the blank with the best word from the choices below. One word will not be used.

   redolent   fetid   stagnant   rancid   olfactory

5. The doctors specializing in ___*olfactory*___ disorders were confused by the patient's inability to smell anything at night.

6. Anna said that the scuffle in the street was hardly ___*redolent*___ of the major brawls that had rocked the town years before.

7. When peeled, the fruit has a(n) ___*fetid*___ odor, like that of old socks.

Fill in the blank with the best word from the choices below. One word will not be used.

   fetid   odoriferous   putrid   rancor   stagnant

8. Scientists studying decomposition delight in ___*putrid*___ matter that other people find disgusting.

9. Paul showed the ___*rancor*___ he had felt for years when he refused to shake my hand.

10. Our ___*stagnant*___ economy seems unable to "wake up," no matter what major events occur.

11. Jackson hated having to drink the ___*odoriferous*___ concoction of vitamins that his mother prepared.

Exercise III. Choose the set of words that best completes the sentence.

1. _____ of the government's long history of internal fighting, the crisis in Congress dragged on; some said the _____ between senators would only grow worse.
   A. rancor; stagnant
   B. olfactory; rancor
   C. putrid; rancor
   D. *redolent; rancor*

2. As she approached the silent, _____ brook, Lakshmi was struck by the smell of something unimaginably _____.
   A. putrid; olfactory
   B. fetid; stagnant
   C. *stagnant; putrid*
   D. malodorous; rancid

3.   "What a _____ candle," sniffed Herman. "It smells like some horrible vegetable has _____ in here."
      A.   putrid; stagnated
      B.   malodorous; putrefied
      C.   olfactory; fetid
      D.   putrid; rancid

4.   In a study of human _____ responses, subjects smelled both fresh and _____ salad dressing.
      A.   malodorous; putrid
      B.   stagnant; fetid
      C.   putrid; stagnant
      D.   olfactory; rancid

5.   When allowed to _____, the canal filled with _____ seaweed that could be smelled for miles.
      A.   stagnate; fetid
      B.   putrefy; olfactory
      C.   rancor; stagnant
      D.   stagnate; olfactory

Exercise IV. Complete the sentence by drawing an inference about the *italicized* word from its context.

Answers will vary by student.

1.   When Mariah says that she is *stagnating* in her current job, we can guess that she would like to…

2.   If Gina says that something in the room must be *rancid*, the expression on her face is probably one of…

3.   A book dealing with *olfactory* disorders will probably be filled with pictures of…

Exercise V. Fill in the blank with the word from the Unit that best completes the sentence, using the root we supply as a clue. Then answer the questions that follow.

In the upcoming "Zombie Night Five," a group of five teenagers is stalked and gradually eliminated by an evil presence that turns them into the living dead. What seems to be a run-of-the-mill slasher flick turns out, on closer observation, to be an intelligent look at some of America's most important issues.

Take, for example, a scene in which Shelby (played by Greta Reese) manages to escape the zombies by finding her way into a toy store with an unlocked back door. There, to her surprise, she finds Zeke (Elijah Mbembe) and Alice (Darlene Knut) already there, they relate their own stories of near-death to her. Arguments arise over what to do. Shelby

suggests that they make a mad dash for a store selling religious artifacts on the upper level of the mall. Alice murmurs fatalistically that they would be better off heading for the ___**malodorous**___ (ODOR) dumpsters behind the mall, thereby at least spoiling the zombies' appetites as they are devoured.

The clever humor of the scene is typical of the film, and the actors deliver their lines with perfect timing. However, its larger message about conflicts between religious believers and nonbelievers—the characters move into a dialogue that I won't spoil for you here—is even more skillfully delivered. Regardless of your views on religion, you will appreciate this film's thoughtful consideration of the "great faith divide."

In addition, the film is chock-a-block with clever pop-culture references and subtle jabs at the "material American" of our time. The setting of the film in the mall is no accident; stores that repeat themselves in shopping centers across America suddenly seem to eat their young clientele, and, in a kind of perverse symbiosis, the kids feed upon the very forces that draw out their lifeblood.

The acting in "Zombie Night Five" is superb. The final twist is fittingly ironic, and certain of the characters undergo complex personality shifts. Even the zombies, their flesh in the process of ___*putrefying*___ (PUTR), are disgusting enough to keep you up at night. All in all, the film is ___*redolent*___ (OL) of the director's early masterpieces, and is destined to become a classic itself.

1. What is the purpose of the second paragraph?
    A. To explain the plot of the movie
    B. *To describe a scene that backs up the author's point*
    C. To summarize the larger message about religious conflicts
    D. To recommend "Zombie Night Five"

2. The tone of this passage could best be described as
    A. *persuasive.*
    B. apologetic.
    C. descriptive.
    D. informative.

3. According to the passage, "Zombie Night Five" is
    A. *like some of the director's early work.*
    B. totally unlike anything the director has ever done.
    C. run-of-the-mill, like the director's early work.
    D. unlike anything the critic has ever seen.

Exercise VI. Drawing on your knowledge of roots and words in context, read the following selection and define the *italicized* words. Note that the suffix *escent* means "growing, increasing."

Answers will vary by student.

Opponents of the new factory have exaggerated its environmental effect. They paint a bleak picture of polluted water in which nothing remains but the *putrescent* remains of animals and plants. In actuality, the factory will have strict safeguards to prevent its harming the surrounding area.

Book I

abbreviate
absent
accept
access
aerate
aeronautic
affect
affection
agent
aggressive
agile
alleviate
announce
armament
astrology
astronomical
aura
aurora
barometer
biped
brevity
campaign
campus
capital
captivate
captive
celebration
celebrity
collaborate
command
comment
common
communicate
compass
compassion
conscience
conserve
constellation
convict
cooperate
corporal
corporation
corps
countless
course
credit
creed
current
cursive
decapitate
decision
deflate
deliver
delude
demand
demented
demilitarized
depend
deposit
describe
diagram

disarm
disaster
discount
disintegrate
distant
domestic
dominate
dominion
donation
donor
effort
elevate
elongate
emancipate
emblem
encamp
engrave
envelop
evaluate
evict
exhilarating
expose
extend
fable
fabulous
factor
feast
festival
festive
fortify
fortress
gradual
grammar
graphic
grave
gravity
hilarity
homicide
hyperventilate
idea
ideal
idealistic
illusion
immune
impersonate
impossible
incredible
inflate
inoperable
insane
inspire
integrate
integrity
intend
interest
invalid
invest
jubilant
jubilee
labor
lax
lease

lever
levitate
liberal
liberate
literal
literate
longitude
lunacy
lunar
lunatic
mandate
manual
manufacture
manuscript
mental
mentality
militant
military
militia
narrate
narrative
object
obliterate
observe
occur
omnipotent
operation
opinion
opinionated
oral
oration
oratory
parable
paragraph
paranoia
pardon
passage
passion
passive
patent
pathetic
patient
pedestal
pedestrian
pendulum
permanent
persona
petrify
possess
precision
present
preserve
pretend
process
program
progress
project
prolong
pronounce
rapid
ravage
ravish

refuge
refugee
regal
regicide
reign
reject
relax
release
remain
respirator
reveal
sanitation
sanity
science
scientific
spirit
state
status
stellar
subscribe
success
suppose
suspend
symbolize
sympathy
terrain
terrestrial
territory
transaction
unveil
valid
value
ventilate
vestment
victor

Book II

abduct
abhor
abundant
accelerate
accumulate
acrophobia
activate
administer
administration
advise
agitate
allergy
amass
ambitious
amputate
annual
anticipate
appreciate
approve
approximate
arrange
aspersion
assault
asset
automatic

automaton
avail
celestial
centennial
chronic
chronology
clarify
clarity
comfort
compass
compose
compute
conceive
condone
conduct
confine
confuse
congratulate
consolidate
constant
contemporary
contract
controversy
convert
cumulative
deceive
decelerate
dedicate
deduct
deify
deity
demarcation
depreciate
deputy
derange
deterrent
diagnosis
differ
digest
disapprove
discourse
disgrace
dislocate
disperse
dispose
durable
duration
edition
elect
enact
enclose
endure
energetic
enforce
ergonomic
evident
exception
excite
exclusive
excursion
executive
exhibit

exhume
expectant
extract
finite
fortitude
gratitude
horrific
horrify
humble
humiliate
humility
hydrophobia
hypothesis
import
important
incite
include
indicate
ingest
inhabit
inscribe
inspect
instant
insular
insulate
insult
intercept
intimidate
invigorate
involve
isolate
issue
journal
legend
locale
marinate
mariner
maritime
massive
method
millennium
minister
ministry
monotheism
nebula
nebulous
neglect
notable
notary
notation
odometer
oppose
optic
optical
optometry
participate
passable
patent
peninsula
period
periodic
phobia

polytheism
precious
prescribe
preside
probation
prognosis
prohibit
prosecution
prosthetic
provide
proximity
ratio
ration
rational
react
recognition
reconnaissance
reduce
redundant
refine
refuse
reinforce
relocate
remarkable
reputation
reside
revise
revolution
revolve
sacred
sacrifice
sanctify
sanctuary
satisfactory
satisfy
sedentary
sequence
single
singular
site
situate
sojourn
solar
solarium
solidarity
solitary
solitude
sparse
statistical
substance
subtract
suffer
suggest
supervise
support
surround
suspicious
syndicate
synergy
synthetic
tempo
temporary
terrify
terrorize

theology
timid
timorous
topic
tradition
transcribe
transfer
transit
universal
utopian
valiant
valor
vigorous
vista

Book III
abjure
abstain
accord
adept
affable
affiliate
affluent
agenda
alias
alienate
allegation
alleviate
alteration
altercation
alternate
amble
ambulatory
amiable
amicable
analogous
animosity
anonymous
antagonist
antagonize
antebellum
antibiotic
antonym
aptitude
aristocracy
assonance
audit
auditory
bellicose
belligerence
benefactor
benevolent
benign
bibliophile
biological
bureaucrat
cadence
casualty
cede
circumspect
cognitive
cognizant
collapse
concession

confound
conjure
consecutive
cordial
corporeal
corpulent
courier
decadent
delegate
denomination
deplete
dialogue
dictum
digress
dilate
diminish
discord
disenchanted
disfigure
dismal
dispel
disposition
dissemble
dissonance
divest
domineering
edict
effigy
elapse
elucidate
enamored
encyclopedic
enjoin
enunciate
equanimity
equilibrium
equitable
exacting
execution
expatriate
expedient
filial
formative
generate
gradualism
herbivorous
homogenized
homologous
homonym
immortalize
impart
impartial
impediment
implement
impose
imprecise
improvise
impulsive
inalienable
inaudible
incantation
incision
inclusive
incognito

inconclusive
inconsequential
incorporate
incur
indecisive
indicted
indomitable
ineffable
inept
infantile
infuse
inhibit
iniquity
injunction
invidious
invoke
leaven
legacy
legislative
legitimize
levity
lucid
magnanimous
magnate
magnetic
magnify
malevolent
malicious
maternal
matriculate
matron
megalomaniacal
megalopolis
megawatt
mellifluous
metabolism
metamorphosis
metaphorical
microanalysis
microscopic
microsecond
miniscule
minute
misinformation
monolithic
monologue
monopolize
moribund
mortify
nomenclature
nominal
noxious
obnoxious
omnivorous
partisan
paternal
patricide
patronize
pedagogue
pedant
pedestrian
perceptible
perjury
pernicious

philanthropy
philosophical
photosynthesis
phototropic
plutocrat
posit
preamble
precept
preclude
predominant
prefigure
privileged
proactive
progenitor
progeny
prohibit
prologue
pronouncement
prospect
protagonist
providential
provocative
rapacious
rapt
recant
recede
recurrent
reform
regress
rejoinder
relapse
relative
renounce
replete
repulsion
resonant
retinue
revival
revoke
semblance
simulate
sophisticate
sophistry
sophomoric
specter
suffuse
superfluous
superlative
surreptitious
susceptible
sustain
symbiosis
synonymous
telephoto
tenacious
theocracy
translucent
travesty
unanimous
uniform
unison
vested
vivacious
vivid

voracious

Book V
abominable
abomination
abrasive
accede
acquiesce
adorn
adventitious
ambient
annex
antecedent
appall
appease
append
applicable
appraise
appreciable
apropos
ascertain
assertion
assortment
attrition
auspices
auspicious
beatific
beatitude
belabor
belletrist
candid
candor
catholic
circuitous
colligate
communal
conferment
conflagration
congested
consign
consort
contort
contravene
contrite
corrosive
décor
decorative
decorous
decorum
demonstrative
denounce
depict
depose
desolate
destine
desultory
detrimental
detritus
discern
discomfit
disconcert
disintegrate
disseminate
distort

divulge
ecstasy
effulgent
elaborate
embellish
emblematic
emeritus
entity
erode
essence
euphoria
excommunicate
exert
expendable
extant
exultant
feasible
febrile
felicity
ferment
flagrant
flamboyant
florid
flourish
flourishing
foment
fortuitous
fulminate
germane
germinal
germinate
gestate
gesticulate
hoi polloi
holistic
hyperbole
hypnopedic
hypnotic
impair
impeccable
impending
implicit
importune
in toto
incandescent
incendiary
incense
incommunicado
incorrigible
inexplicable
infelicitous
inflammatory
insignia
insufferable
insurrection
integral
interject
interpose
jocular
jocund
laborious
leniency
lenient
lethargy
liaison

liturgy
magnum opus
malaise
malfeasance
malign
malinger
meritorious
meretricious
misfortune
modus operandi
monosyllabic
monotone
monotonous
munificent
negate
negligent
negligible
nexus
objectify
oblige
ominous
operational
ornate
orthodox
orthography
pacific
pallid
pallor
parcel
parse
parvenu
peccadillo
pejorative
periphery
picturesque
polygamous
polyglot
precedent
predestined
preferential
problematic
propitiate
propitious
quintessence
rapport
raze
rectify
refulgent
remonstrate
remunerate
renounce
repartee
requiem
resignation
resilient
restive
sedition
seminal
serenade
serene
serenity
soliloquy
solipsism
somnambulant

somnolent
sortilege
stanch
stasis
static
staunch
suborn
surfeit
surveillance
suspend
synergy
totalitarian
totality
transient
transitional
transitory
trite
verdant
verdure
vigil
vigilant
vigilante
vulgar

Book VI
abscond
abstruse
adduce
adjourn
adjudicate
adroit
adumbrate
aggregate
agrarian
allocate
allude
amoral
anachronism
animadversion
aperture
apocryphal
apposite
apprise
artifice
artless
ascribe
assay
asset
attenuate
avocation
bucolic
capitulate
caprice
chronicle
circumlocution
circumscribe
cogent
cognate
colloquy
collusion
complicit
composite
comprise
concede

concordance
concur
confluence
conjugal
consecrate
consign
conspire
constrain
contend
contiguous
contingent
covert
cryptic
curative
defray
degenerate
demise
demur
demure
derisive
devoid
diabolical
discern
discordant
discrete
discretion
discursive
distend
diurnal
dour
duplicitous
duress
dystopian
egregious
emblematic
emulate
engender
ensue
episodic
esprit
evanescent
execrable
exigent
expiate
explicate
extemporaneous
extenuating
feign
felicitate
felicity
fictive
flux
genre
gregarious
hyperbole
icon
iconoclast
iconographic
idyllic
impious
implicate
in lieu of
in loco parentis
inanimate

incessant
incite
inconsolable
incorrigible
incurable
inert
inexplicable
infelicitous
influx
infrangible
inimitable
innate
innocuous
insatiable
insuperable
integral
intercede
interlude
internecine
interpose
intransigent
intrusive
inveigh
irrepressible
judicious
locus
loquacious
ludicrous
magniloquent
methodical
moratorium
mores
morose
myopic
nascent
obdurate
obloquy
obsequious
obtrusive
ostensible
overt
pastoral
peregrination
pernicious
pertinacious
perturb
plenary
plenipotentiary
portend
posit
precipitate
prize
procure
proscribe
proverbial
proviso
pysche
pyschosomatic
purveyor
purview
pusillanimous
recapitulate
recondite
rectify

rectitude
remit
repast
reprimand
reserved
resignation
resuscitate
reticent
retinue
risible
rustic
sacrosanct
salubrious
salutary
salutation
satiety
sectarian
segue
servile
signatory
sinecure
sojourn
solace
solicitous
sovereign
stricture
stringent
subdue
subjugate
subservient
succor
suffrage
suppress
surfeit
surmise
synchronous
synod
synopsis
tacit
taciturn
temporal
temporize
tenable
tendentious
tenet
tenuous
topical
traduce
transect
transfigure
transpire
turbid
turbulent
umbrage
utopian
vacuity
vacuous
vaunted
vehement
verbatim
verbiage
verbose
vocation
vociferous

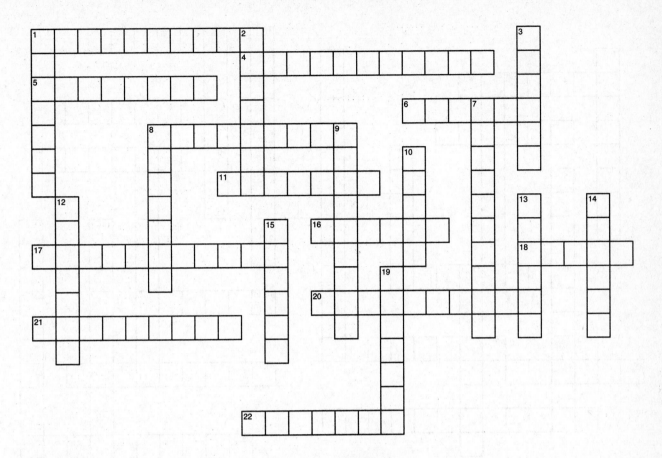

ACROSS

- **1** Unable to be conquered
- **4** To increase greatly in number; multiply
- **5** Irritable or short-tempered
- **6** Cause for action
- **8** Claimed as true, but probably false
- **11** To draw back; withdraw
- **16** To force or strongly persuade; coerce
- **17** Feeling of regret or remorse
- **18** A recurring theme, subject or idea
- **20** Unable to be affected
- **21** Act or practice of yielding to another's authority
- **22** Brief and straightforward

DOWN

- **1** That which drives one; momentum
- **2** The best or most typical example
- **3** Lowly, miserable and wretched
- **7** Minor violation of a rule or law
- **8** Stinging or biting, especially in taste or smell
- **9** Two opposite parts of one whole
- **10** To send out or away
- **12** To present or offer
- **13** Failing to fulfill one's duty; negligent
- **14** To establish; to reflect the truth of
- **15** To lead towards some action
- **19** To depart, especially from a path or plan

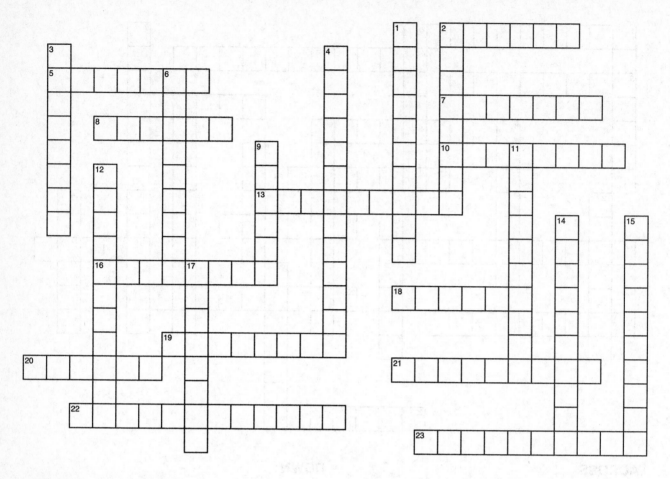

ACROSS

2 Easily taught; submissive to instruction
5 Plentiful; abundant
7 One who is not properly thankful
8 Calm; undisturbed
10 To imagine; to conceive of
13 One who argues in favor of; supporter
16 Existing as a natural part
18 To decrease the strength of
19 To interpret or analyze something in a particular way
20 Too simplistic or easy
21 Having no money; poor
22 To teach a certain point of view to
23 Lightweight and transparent

DOWN

1 Skilled at; highly knowledgeable of
2 Hard-working and careful
3 A moment of great insight; revelation
4 Looking backward over a period of time
6 An act against a holy person or place
9 A part that can be considered or viewed
11 Not able to be understood; nonsensical
12 Payment for an injury; compensation
14 An unreal figure; a ghost
15 Unnecessary or unwanted
17 Determined; steadfast

REVIEW EXERCISE - UNITS 9-12

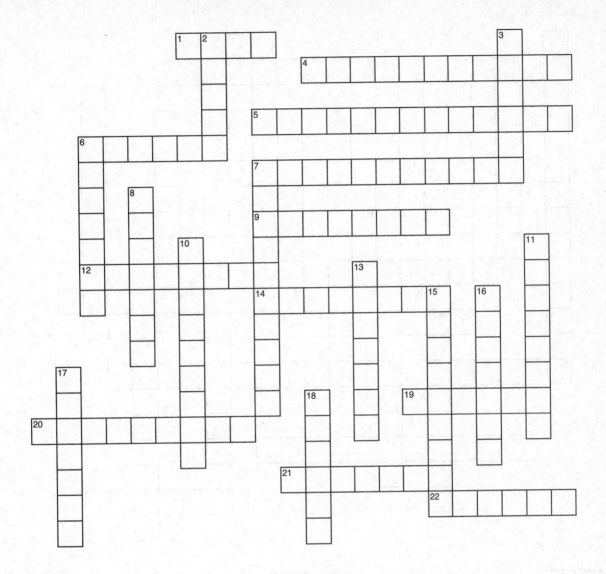

ACROSS

1 Burden or obligation
4 Unable to believe something; amazed
5 To do away with legal penalties for
6 Original; dating from the beginning of existence
7 Certain beyond doubt or question
9 Faithfulness; loyalty
12 Trust or belief
14 Deserving blame
19 To respond critically or sarcastically
20 A demand or threat that is final
21 To cause to turn aside or away
22 To unfold; to develop or change gradually

DOWN

2 New and different
3 An inexperienced person; amateur
6 Condition of being first in time or importance
7 Change in pitch or tone of the voice
8 Not helpful; harmful
10 A dishonest or immoral person; a scoundrel
11 Without beginning or end
13 A misleading or mistaken idea
15 To prove not guilty
16 Uncertain; doubtful
17 One responsible for a crime
18 To fall back into an old condition

REVIEW EXERCISE - UNITS 13-16

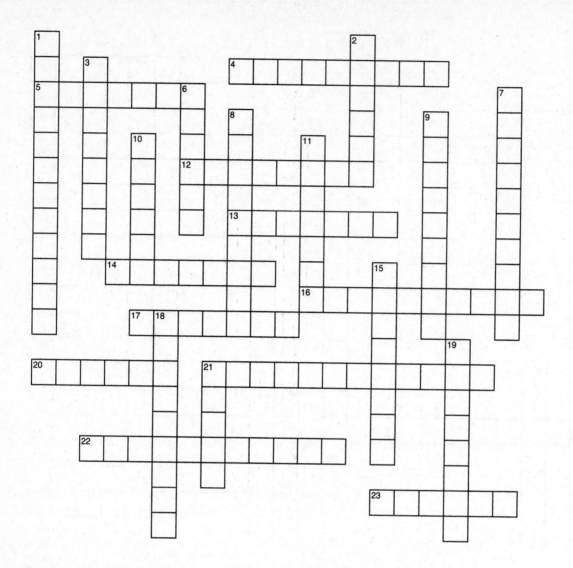

ACROSS

4 Characterized by a loud noise or outcry
5 To call together, to assemble
12 Powerful and expressive
13 Harsh and biting in tone
14 To speak loudly and with feeling
16 To use misleading or confusing language
17 Passionately excited or enthusiastic
20 Emotional excitement; heated enthusiasm
21 Worldly or sophisticated
22 A recital of words intended to harm; a curse
23 Masculine; manly

DOWN

1 Extremely painful; agonizing
2 Wandering or straying
3 Lazy; averse to work
6 Act of going out; exit
7 To make worse or more severe
8 Calling forth a vivid image or impression
9 That which comes before; forerunner
10 Right action; moral goodness
11 To lower in dignity or esteem; insult
15 Politeness; courteousness
18 Wrong or inaccurate
19 Having an effect on a large area or region
21 Having to do with the business of a town or community

Reproducible Student Worksheet

REVIEW EXERCISE - UNITS 17-19

ACROSS

1 To be similar to; compare to
4 Sharing of another's emotions
7 Excessively proud; haughty
9 Lacking all hope
11 Having to do with beauty or order
13 Unbroken; whole
14 Not based on reason or logic
17 Conscious; aware
18 A feeling about something
19 Threatened or unsafe
20 To assign blame or responsibility for
21 Insulting; degrading

DOWN

2 To support; pledge support to
3 To explain or discuss through a note
5 Not interested; having no strong emotion towards
6 An image or idea associated with a word
8 Diligent and careful
10 A reason for doing something; explanation
12 Curious; asking many questions
15 Able to be grasped or perceived
16 Showing knowledge of events before they happen

ACROSS

5 Acceptable; satisfactory

7 Enthusiastic enjoyment

8 Gentle scolding

11 An action taken against danger ahead of time

12 Too much of something; oversupply

15 Drink; soak up

16 Enthusiastic; eager

17 Having an unpleasant smell

18 Giving off an odor

20 Careful not to get into danger

21 Intended to lessen another's anger

DOWN

1 To convince one not to do something

2 Unhealthy because of lack of movement

3 Suggesting; carrying the hint of

4 To bring back into agreement

6 Bitterness; hostility

9 Dull; uninteresting

10 Rotten; suggesting decomposition

13 Habit or type

14 Having to do with the sense of smell

19 Taste or liking

Solution:

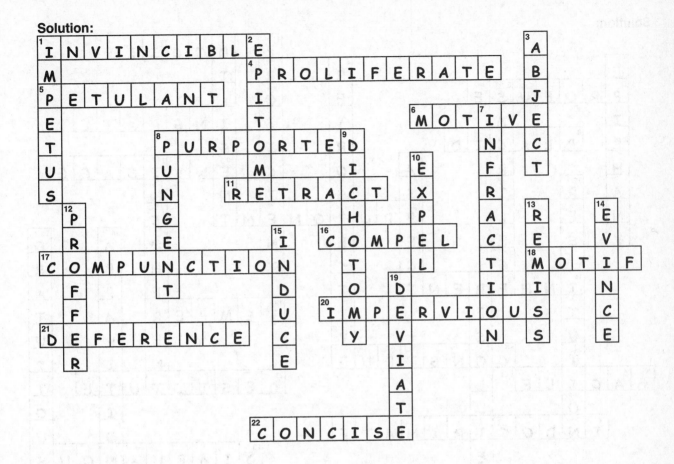

ACROSS

1 Unable to be conquered
4 To increase greatly in number; multiply
5 Irritable or short-tempered
6 Cause for action
8 Claimed as true, but probably false
11 To draw back; withdraw
16 To force or strongly persuade; coerce
17 Feeling of regret or remorse
18 A recurring theme, subject or idea
20 Unable to be affected
21 Act or practice of yielding to another's authority
22 Brief and straightforward

DOWN

1 That which drives one; momentum
2 The best or most typical example
3 Lowly, miserable and wretched
7 Minor violation of a rule or law
8 Stinging or biting, especially in taste or smell
9 Two opposite parts of one whole
10 To send out or away
12 To present or offer
13 Failing to fulfill one's duty; negligent
14 To establish; to reflect the truth of
15 To lead towards some action
19 To depart, especially from a path or plan

Solution:

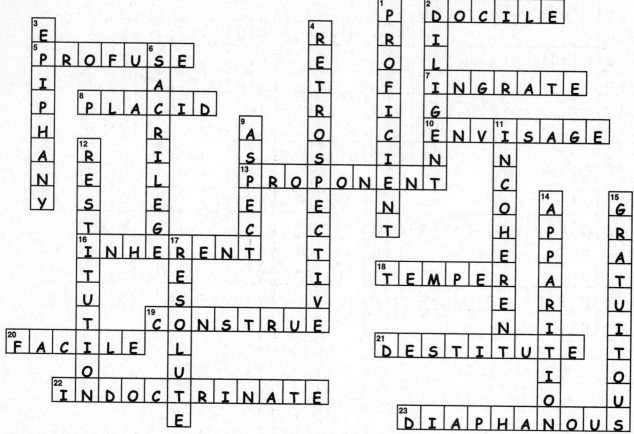

ACROSS

2 Easily taught; submissive to instruction
5 Plentiful; abundant
7 One who is not properly thankful
8 Calm; undisturbed
10 To imagine; to conceive of
13 One who argues in favor of; supporter
16 Existing as a natural part
18 To decrease the strength of
19 To interpret or analyze something in a particular way
20 Too simplistic or easy
21 Having no money; poor
22 To teach a certain point of view to
23 Lightweight and transparent

DOWN

1 Skilled at; highly knowledgeable of
2 Hard-working and careful
3 A moment of great insight; revelation
4 Looking backward over a period of time
6 An act against a holy person or place
9 A part that can be considered or viewed
11 Not able to be understood; nonsensical
12 Payment for an injury; compensation
14 An unreal figure; a ghost
15 Unnecessary or unwanted
17 Determined; steadfast

REVIEW EXERCISE ANSWER KEY - UNITS 9-12

Solution:

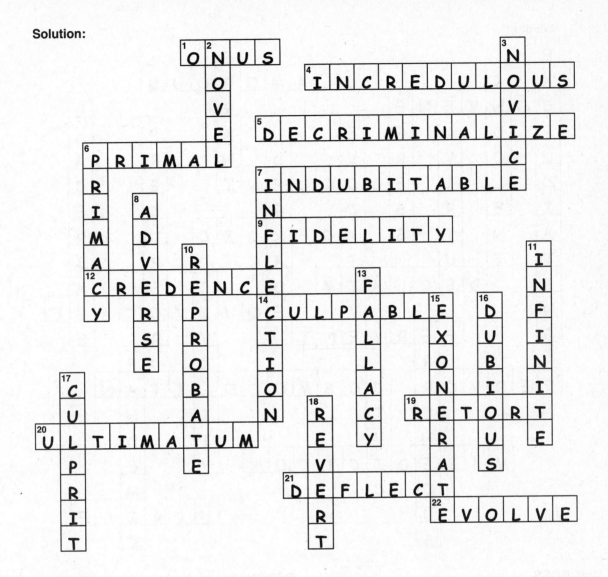

ACROSS

1 Burden or obligation
4 Unable to believe something; amazed
5 To do away with legal penalties for
6 Original; dating from the beginning of existence
7 Certain beyond doubt or question
9 Faithfulness; loyalty
12 Trust or belief
14 Deserving blame
19 To respond critically or sarcastically
20 A demand or threat that is final
21 To cause to turn aside or away
22 To unfold; to develop or change gradually

DOWN

2 New and different
3 An inexperienced person; amateur
6 Condition of being first in time or importance
7 Change in pitch or tone of the voice
8 Not helpful; harmful
10 A dishonest or immoral person; a scoundrel
11 Without beginning or end
13 A misleading or mistaken idea
15 To prove not guilty
16 Uncertain; doubtful
17 One responsible for a crime
18 To fall back into an old condition

Solution:

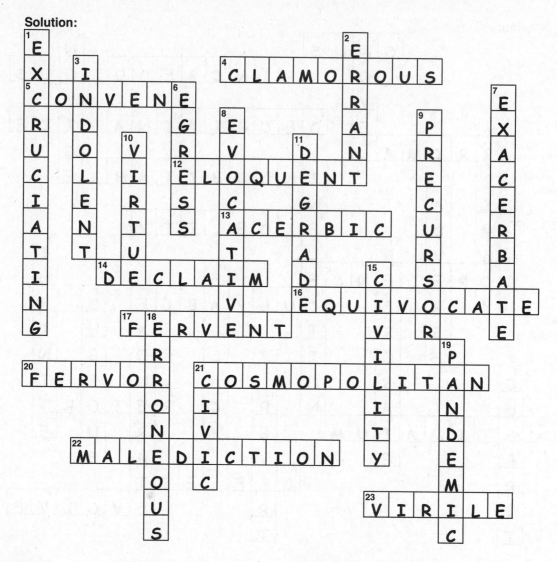

ACROSS

4 Characterized by a loud noise or outcry
5 To call together, to assemble
12 Powerful and expressive
13 Harsh and biting in tone
14 To speak loudly and with feeling
16 To use misleading or confusing language
17 Passionately excited or enthusiastic
20 Emotional excitement; heated enthusiasm
21 Worldly or sophisticated
22 A recital of words intended to harm; a curse
23 Masculine; manly

DOWN

1 Extremely painful; agonizing
2 Wandering or straying
3 Lazy; averse to work
6 Act of going out; exit
7 To make worse or more severe
8 Calling forth a vivid image or impression
9 That which comes before; forerunner
10 Right action; moral goodness
11 To lower in dignity or esteem; insult
15 Politeness; courteousness
18 Wrong or inaccurate
19 Having an effect on a large area or region
21 Having to do with the business of a town or community

Solution:

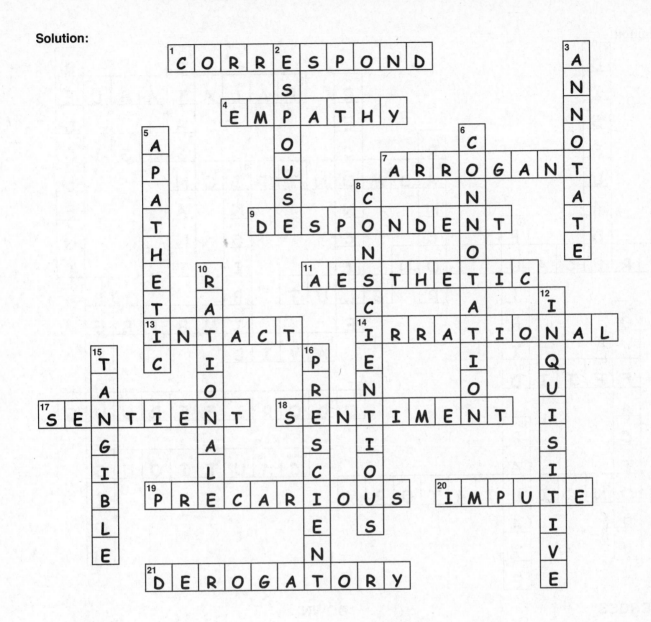

ACROSS

1 To be similar to; compare to
4 Sharing of another's emotions
7 Excessively proud; haughty
9 Lacking all hope
11 Having to do with beauty or order
13 Unbroken; whole
14 Not based on reason or logic
17 Conscious; aware
18 A feeling about something
19 Threatened or unsafe
20 To assign blame or responsibility for
21 Insulting; degrading

DOWN

2 To support; pledge support to
3 To explain or discuss through a note
5 Not interested; having no strong emotion towards
6 An image or idea associated with a word
8 Diligent and careful
10 A reason for doing something; explanation
12 Curious; asking many questions
15 Able to be grasped or perceived
16 Showing knowledge of events before they happen

Solution:

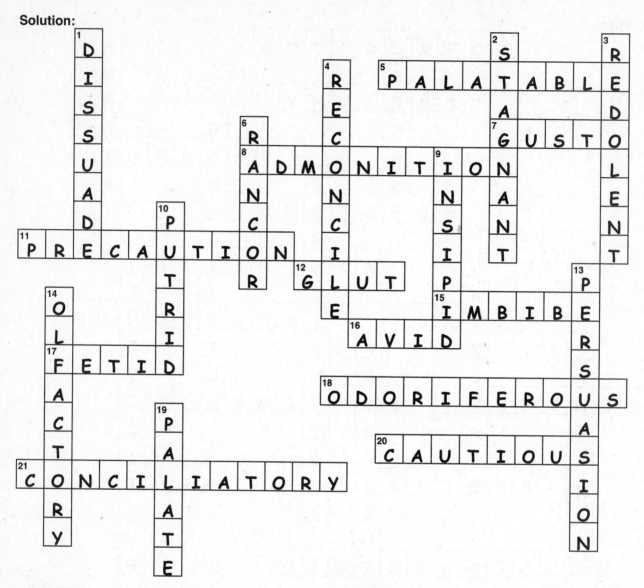

ACROSS

5 Acceptable; satisfactory
7 Enthusiastic enjoyment
8 Gentle scolding
11 An action taken against danger ahead of time
12 Too much of something; oversupply
15 Drink; soak up
16 Enthusiastic; eager
17 Having an unpleasant smell
18 Giving off an odor
20 Careful not to get into danger
21 Intended to lessen another's anger

DOWN

1 To convince one not to do something
2 Unhealthy because of lack of movement
3 Suggesting; carrying the hint of
4 To bring back into agreement
6 Bitterness; hostility
9 Dull; uninteresting
10 Rotten; suggesting decomposition
13 Habit or type
14 Having to do with the sense of smell
19 Taste or liking

Dramatically Improve Student Writing with our Powerful New Writing Program!

3 Simple Truths and 6 Essential Traits of Powerful Writing™

- Improve student test scores
- Unify your school's writing curriculum
- Provide clear goals for your students
- Track development across grade levels
- Build a clear process for monitoring student progress
- Make the abstract process of grading writing more concrete

Once you've seen how students can develop from novice writers to proficient, powerful writers through our highly organized system, you'll wonder how you ever taught writing before.

In developing this program, we've focused on the needs of today's teachers. *3 Simple Truths and 6 Essential Traits of Powerful Writing*,™ provides teachers with a clear framework for teaching and evaluating writing, including a starting and ending point for each grade, a wide variety of writing prompts and exercises, and concrete guidelines for the difficult job of grading subjective essays.

The clarity of objectives provided by the unique 14-point rubric will help your students fully understand not only their current status, but also what they need to do in order to improve.

No Risk Guarantee!

We guarantee that you've never seen a more effective writing program—and we'll prove it with this unprecedented guarantee. Buy a class set of books with the accompanying CD for $240.00; then, use the program for an entire year. If you don't agree that it's the best program available, return the battered, bruised, soiled, and marked material, and we'll refund your purchase price of $240.00, plus shipping. *There's nothing to lose!*

Introductory Price!

Book I: Novice Level

X301633	Class Set of 30 Books and CD Teacher's Guide	~~$299.99~~	$240.00
X301612	Single Copy	~~$10.95~~	$8.95

Book II: Developing Level

X301634	Class Set of 30 Books and CD Teacher's Guide	~~$299.99~~	$240.00
X301613	Single Copy	~~$10.95~~	$8.95

Book III: Advancing Level

X301635	Class Set of 30 Books and CD Teacher's Guide	~~$299.99~~	$240.00
X301614	Single Copy	~~$10.95~~	$8.95

Book IV: Proficient Level

X301636	Class Set of 30 Books and CD Teacher's Guide	~~$299.99~~	$240.00
X301615	Single Copy	~~$10.95~~	$8.95

Call Toll Free: **1.800.932.4593**
FAX 24/7 at **1.888.718.9333**

PH PRESTWICK HOUSE, INC.
"Everything for the English Classroom!"

Visit us online at
www.prestwickhouse.com